Leckie×Leckie

Scotland's leading educational publishers

D1407242

National 5
BUSINESS MANAGEMENT
SUCCESS GUIDE

Anne Ross

001/29072013

ISBN 9780007504947

Published by
Leckie & Leckie Ltd
An imprint of HarperCollins*Publishers*
Westerhill Road, Bishopbriggs, Glasgow, G64 2QT
T: 0844 576 8126   F: 0844 576 8131
leckieandleckie@harpercollins.co.uk   www.leckieandleckie.co.uk

Special thanks to
Donna Cole (copyeditor and proofreader)
Delphine Lawrance (picture research)
Q2A Bill Smith (layout)
Pam Oates (content review)

A CIP Catalogue record for this book is available from the British Library.

Acknowledgements
We would like to thank the following for permission to reproduce their
material:
Car production photo on page 14 © Nataliya Hora/Shutterstock.com; RBS logo
on page 17 courtesy of RBS; SCVO logo on page 22 courtesy of the Scottish
Council for Voluntary Organisations; Photo of high street on page 26 © Chris
Green/Shutterstock.com; Photo of protest on page 31 © Albert H. Teich/
Shutterstock.com; Photo of the Scottish parliament on page 32 © Jeff J Mitchell/
Getty Images; Photo of music festival on page 33 © Christian Bertrand/
Shutterstock.com; Photo of lecture on page 38 © Pavel L Photo and Video/
Shutterstock.com; Photo of protest on page 42 © i4cocl2/Shutterstock.com;
Photo of production line on page 55 © Bartolomiej Magierowski/Shutterstock.
com; Ford logo on page 67 courtesy of Ford; Cadbury logo on page 67
courtesy of Cadbury; Photo of tea picking on page 78 © Simon Rawles;
FAIRTRADE Mark logo on page 78 courtesy of Fairtrade International; Photo of
cans being recycled on page 80 © Huguette Roe/Shutterstock.com

All other images from Shutterstock

Whilst every effort has been made to trace the copyright holders, in cases
where this has been unsuccessful, or if any have inadvertently been overlooked,
the Publishers would gladly receive any information enabling them to rectify
any error or omission at the first opportunity.

Contents

Getting Started

Understanding Business

Contents

Management of People and Finance

Management of Marketing and Operations

The Business Management Course

About this *Success Guide*

This book has been written to help you succeed in the National 5 Business Management course. Throughout this course you will gain knowledge and understanding of business concepts, as well as an understanding of people and finance, marketing and operations. You will develop skills and learn how to apply these skills.

Throughout this book you will see Exam Tips, Develop Your Skills, Apply Your Knowledge and Quick Tests as well as recaps of all the topics you have studied.

- Exam Tips have advice that should help you both during your course and for the exam and assignment. You should pay careful attention to these.

- Develop Your Skills sections help you to apply your knowledge and understanding in order to develop your skills in literacy, numeracy, decision-making, research, communication etc.

- Apply Your Knowledge sections are designed to get you thinking about some of the issues raised in the chapters. The answers to these sections are not always straightforward; you will have to think about the particular situation you are being asked about.

- Quick Tests are designed to get you thinking as you work through this *Success Guide*. All the answers are provided for you from page 76 onwards.

Assessment

National 5 Business Management has three units and a course assessment.
- **Unit 1** – Understanding Business
- **Unit 2** – Management of People and Finance
- **Unit 3** – Management of Marketing and Operations

Unit assessment

Each of the three units will be assessed separately in the classroom and the format of the assessment for each unit will vary. Your teacher should make it very clear to you *when and how you are being assessed*. It may take the form of a written test or you may be assessed as part of a group task. What is very important, however, is that you always use **business terminology** and that you include **real business examples** where possible.

> **EXAM TIP**
>
> From the beginning of your course you should always use proper business terminology. It would be helpful to create your own glossary of business words and phrases.

The course assessment

The course assessment has two components:

Component 1 is an exam question paper that is worth 70 marks. This question paper has two sections.

- **Section 1** is worth 30 marks and consists of short answer questions based on stimulus material usually based on a real-life or realistic business.

- **Section 2** is worth 40 marks and consists of questions that require extended responses. There will be a choice of questions in this section. Questions in this section can be from any part of the course.

Component 2 is an assignment worth 30 marks; it is undertaken in class but is externally marked by the SQA. The assignment topic is set by the SQA and is split into two parts: research and write-up. During class time you will undertake the appropriate research and keep a careful record of all your findings. Once this research is complete you will write-up your research under supervised conditions.

> **EXAM TIP**
>
> It is really important that you keep all your research findings organised, particularly when recording any websites that you have used. You do not want to waste time having to repeat your research.

The course assessment

Introduction

In order to pass your Business Management course you have to sit an exam paper and complete an assignment. This chapter gives you advice about both. You can study for the final exam in a variety of different ways that suit your learning style. Some examples are given below. You cannot study in the same way for the assignment, but there is advice below on how to approach it.

How do I prepare for the exam?

Gather together all your resources from your Business Management course. It could be your notes, this *Success Guide*, textbooks, website printouts, class tests etc. Make a note of the main topic areas that you wish to study first. For each topic area, decide which study techniques you are going to use, for example:

- make a list of keywords
- use a mind map
- try a past paper question
- listen to a relevant podcast
- prepare a poster
- highlight notes and texts
- work with a friend on Q&A sessions
- use a website

Decide on the time you are going to allocate to revising each topic, taking into account your own attention span. It is advisable to take short regular breaks and to drink plenty of water to keep focused.

The question paper (exam paper)

Section 1 has stimulus material. There are other names given to this, such as case study, passage etc. This is usually based on a real business or a realistic business. The following steps will help you answer the questions.

1. Read the stimulus material carefully.

2. Read the questions to get an overall feeling for what is being asked.

3. Re-read the stimulus materials and look for key business words or phrases that will help you answer the question. Highlight these if it helps you.

4. Answer each question in turn, paying attention to the command words.

Section 2 has extended response questions. These questions cover all topics from the course and there is some choice. Choose questions that you know you can answer in depth. Highlight the command words in the question so that you are very clear about what you are being asked to do. Pay particular attention to the marks allocated to each question. Your answers should be as full as possible, with proper sentences. Bullet points are acceptable for some command words, which are explained on the next page.

Command words

The command words in the table below are examples of those used frequently in external examinations. You should pay particular attention to the command words used in any assessment you undertake.

Command word	Definition
Compare	Identify similarities and differences between two or more factors.
Define	Give a clear meaning.
Describe	Provide a thorough description.
Distinguish	Identify the differences between two or more factors. Remember to use where/but/however.
Explain	Give details about how and why something is as it is.
Give	Pick some key factors and name them.
Identify	Give the name or identifying characteristics of something.
Name	Identify or make a list.
Outline	State the main features. This needs more detail than just a list.
Suggest	State a possible reason or course of action (no development required).

The assignment

You will complete the assignment in class, and it gives you a degree of personalisation and choice. The SQA will provide the topics for the assignment. This will be your opportunity to apply the knowledge, understanding and skills you have learned throughout the course in order to solve a business problem or to advise a business about how to become more effective.

Once you have chosen your topic you will be able to research that business using a range of sources, for example:

- the company website
- other websites
- newspapers, journals and magazines
- advertising leaflets or advertisements on TV
- DVDs or videos from the Internet
- field trips or visiting speakers

Once you have gathered the information you need, you must analyse the data and come up with conclusions or recommendations about how the business can improve. What is important here is that you use your business knowledge in the context of the business you have chosen.

You will have to justify your recommendations. This can be the tricky bit as you have to be able to give good reasons, which are usually based on the following:

* why have you made this recommendation?
* is there an alternative?
* what will the consequences be if the business carries out your recommendations?
* what will the consequences be if the business does not carry out your recommendations?

Skills development

Skills for learning, skills for life and skills for work

Every course that you undertake as part of your education should develop skills that employers are looking for, and also skills that will help you progress in your life outside work. We all need skills in literacy and numeracy. In addition, we also need to be able to think for ourselves and to show that we are employable. The Business Management course will help you to develop a range of skills.

Literacy in business management

You can develop and improve your literacy skills in a number of different ways.

- Watching business news and making short notes.
- Reading about business in newspapers or on Internet websites.
- Making a presentation about a business you have researched.
- Having a discussion in class.
- Composing business documents, such as job descriptions, advertisements for a product, etc.
- Taking part in a role play, for example a job interview.
- Compiling a business glossary.

Numeracy in business management

You can develop and improve your numeracy skills in a number of different ways.

- Calculating profits and losses.
- Preparing a cash budget.
- Entering formula into a spreadsheet for financial transactions.
- Preparing a chart or graph.
- Using financial information to make decisions.

Employability, Enterprise and Citizenship in business management

Everyone hopes to get a job when they finish their education. For some, this is straight from school, for others this is after further or higher education. Whenever you hope to get a job, employers always look for certain skills. Are you employable?

The Business Management course can help you develop skills that employers are looking for. You will be employable if you can:

- show some understanding of how businesses work
- show initiative in your work, for example undertaking research and solving problems
- communicate effectively both in person and using ICT
- demonstrate leadership skills
- come up with ideas to help the business improve
- protect the environment through recycling and re-using
- understand the laws that businesses have to work within, such as equality or health and safety legislation

Thinking skills

The Business Management course can help you to think about problems and how to solve them.

Employers want you to be able to think rather than just learning facts. We all have to think for ourselves on a daily basis, but in business management this can take many different forms.

- Using the correct business terminology.
- Researching a business problem and suggesting how to solve it.
- Planning, organising and completing business tasks.
- Working with others to link your ideas together.
- Using the Internet with critical appreciation: do you always trust the information on the website?
- Making decisions, giving recommendations and justifications.

Other skills in business management

The Business Management course will only be successful if by the end you can say that you have the ability to:

- make decisions based on relevant information
- communicate with others both in person and using ICT
- research, interpret and evaluate information to solve problems
- demonstrate enterprising skills and attitudes

EXAM TIP

Skills are important in our modern society. For example, anyone can find basic information on the Internet – it is what you do with that information that makes you enterprising and successful.

Satisfying wants

Needs and wants

Being a human means that we have needs and wants. In our modern society we aim to satisfy our needs and wants in many different ways. However, basic human needs are just about the same for everyone. We all need clean water, food, clothing, shelter. Everyone has wants but they are relative to whether you are in the UK or in Bangladesh. In the UK our wants far surpass the basic minimum needs. People in developing countries are not so fortunate.

Wants include luxuries such as computers, fashion, mobile phones, fast cars, luxury holidays etc.

Businesses provide us with our needs and wants. They provide the products (goods) we want to buy and pay for. Some businesses also provide us with services, for example hairdressers, restaurants, banks or transport companies. Once we have used up these goods and services we expect businesses to provide them again. This is known as **consumption**. Businesses not only provide goods, services and jobs, they also create wealth for our society.

The factors of production

Businesses provide goods and services by combining the four factors of production: **land**, **labour**, **capital** and **enterprise**.

Land	This includes all the natural resources of the earth, as well as the physical land that a business is located on.
Labour	Men and women who make up the workforce for any business or organisation.
Capital	Machines, equipment and resources used in the business. It also includes cash (money) to start-up the business.
Enterprise	The idea behind the business, usually provided by an entrepreneur. Without the enterprising idea there wouldn't be a business.

Creating wealth

Businesses create wealth by adding value to products as they go through the various stages in the production process. For example, a carpenter who makes handcrafted wooden furniture will add value in the following way:

- the forest owner sells wood to the sawmill for £30
- the sawmill cuts and treats the wood and sells it to the carpenter for £65
- the carpenter carves the wood into a table and sells the finished table for £150

Throughout the process, wealth has been created to the value of £120.

EXAM TIP

Wealth is created by businesses adding value at each stage of the production process.

Apply Your Knowledge

Describe how wealth would be created in each of the following production scenarios.
- Ford making cars.
- A hairdresser's business.
- BP producing petrol.

Develop Your Skills

Describe the factors of production in each of the following business contexts.
- Making designer jeans.
- Producing a magazine.
- Building a new home.

Quick Test

| 1. | Describe the difference between needs and wants. |
| 2. | Describe how wealth is created by a business. |

Sectors of industry and the economy

Sectors of industry

In the previous lesson the production of the table by the carpenter illustrates the different stages that products go through, these stages are known as the **sectors of industry**. There are three sectors of industry: **primary**, **secondary** and **tertiary.**

The primary sector

The primary sector involves taking raw materials from the natural habitat. These raw materials are then passed to the next sector in the production process. Examples of businesses operating in the primary sector are farming, oil extraction, fishing and quarrying.

The secondary sector

This involves taking raw materials and making them into finished products, and is often called **manufacturing**. Examples of businesses operating in the secondary sector are: manufacturers of products such as washing machines, cars, food or computers.

The tertiary sector

This involves providing a service. Examples of businesses operating in the tertiary sector are hairdressers, banks, travel agents, schools, dentists etc.

Sectors of the economy

As well as operating in a particular sector of industry, businesses and organisations also operate within a particular **sector of the economy**: the **private sector**, the **public sector** or the **third sector**.

The public sector

The public sector of the economy is owned and controlled by the government and local councils. It provides services such as schools, hospitals, the armed forces

and social services. These are funded by taxes. These are usually referred to as organisations or public bodies rather than businesses.

The private sector

This sector of the economy is owned and controlled by private individuals and is made up of types of businesses known as sole traders, partnerships, limited companies, franchises etc. They are funded by private individuals and shareholders.

The third sector

This is made up of charities and other community organisations that aim to raise money for good causes and to help people. The third sector also includes social enterprises and co-operatives. They are not 'owned' by anyone: they raise money from donations, fundraising activities and grants from the lottery.

> **EXAM TIP**
> It is important than you can distinguish between sectors of **industry** and sectors of the **economy**.

Apply Your Knowledge

Identify the sector of industry that each of the following businesses operates in.

- Clydesdale Bank
- American Airlines
- Ford Cars
- BP

Develop Your Skills

Identify four businesses in your local area or an area that you are familiar with.

- What goods or services do they provide?
- What sector of industry do they operate in?
- Are they a large or small business?
- What sector of the economy do they belong to?

Quick Test

1. Name the three sectors of industry.
2. Give an example of an organisation that operates in the public sector.

What is customer service?

Customer service involves using a range of techniques in order to keep customers happy. However keeping customers happy is not an easy task.

- What does 'being happy' mean?
- Do all customers want the same level of service?

What keeps one customer happy might not suit another customer.

Finding out if customers are happy

Businesses and organisations must have systems in place for receiving feedback from customers on their products and services. Feedback can take the form of **market research** or giving customers the opportunity to submit their comments via websites, customer service telephone lines, video booths, in-store comment cards etc.

The importance of good customer service

Many businesses recognise the importance of good customer service – therefore they are prepared to spend time and money investing in good staff and training. If customers are happy then the business will benefit in many ways, such as:

- increased customer loyalty
- increased sales and profits
- a good reputation
- increased competitiveness
- increased staff morale and effectiveness

Customers who feel they are treated well and get good service will be happy to return to the business. They will also pass this on to others, with the potential of increasing customers for the business overall.

Customer loyalty

To keep customers loyal and ensure they return to the business, a business should provide the same standard or a higher standard of products and services at competitive prices. Over and above this, the business should regularly update the product or service in line with customers' needs and feedback. In addition, the business should be proactive and step-in first when something goes wrong to make sure that customers feel they are important.

Staff training

The business or organisation must train all employees in customer service. Employees need to make sure that they are sensitive to customers' needs and wants and know how to satisfy them. Many businesses approach this from a **quality management** perspective, or they try and gain awards in customer service and excellence. Quality management means that every single employee in the business is trained in customer service and knows the importance of keeping customers happy.

> **EXAM TIP**
>
> Good customer service does not happen by accident! Staff have to be carefully trained to make sure that each and every customer gets the experience they are looking for and will return to the business.

Setting service standards

Many businesses and organisations will set customer service standards. These often quantify timelines and expectations, such as how long the telephone should ring before being answered or how long it should take to answer an email or a letter. Another approach is to offer 'extras' with the product being purchased, for example including free servicing or a car wash every 2 weeks with a new car purchase.

As an example of this, the bank RBS has created a customer charter that outlines quite specific customer service targets. It then publishes an annual report on how it meets these targets.

Apply Your Knowledge

What would you include in a customer care policy for a fast food restaurant such as Pizza Hut, McDonalds or Frankie and Benny's?

Develop Your Skills

Read the RBS Customer Charter at www.rbs.co.uk. In the past, RBS have said 'we will serve 90% of customers in five minutes or less in our branches'. How do you think they can measure this? What will they do if customers are not served during this time?

Quick Test

1.	Describe two ways that businesses can offer customers good service.
2.	Give three reasons for offering good customer service.
3.	Explain why it is important to train staff in customer service.

Complaints, refunds and guarantees

Complaints procedure

Customers need to be assured that not only can they complain if they are not happy, but more importantly that something will be done about their complaint. Each business or organisation should have an established complaints procedure. This can take the form of a dedicated telephone service, in-store customer desk or a website feedback form.

Refund and exchange policy

A returns policy will give information about refunds and exchanges of goods and should contain at least the following information:

- whether the business gives refunds, exchanges goods or offers other forms of compensation
- the maximum time after purchase that refunds or exchanges are given
- the type of refund given

All staff should know the details of this policy and it should be clearly visible to customers at all times. Customers should have confidence in the policy.

Guarantees

Businesses and organisations can offer **guarantees** to customers, but the conditions of these guarantees should be achievable and very clearly explained. For example, airline companies cannot guarantee that all aircraft will take off and land on time but they can guarantee the cleanliness of the aircraft and the customer service approach adopted by their staff. Guarantees can apply to the **physical condition** of products, for example guaranteeing a replacement if a purchase stops working. Guarantees can also apply to **standards**, for example the guaranteed delivery times of an online purchase or the qualifications of a driving instructor, etc.

Apply Your Knowledge

What would you do in the following situations?

- A customer complains that their meal in the restaurant is lukewarm.
- A customer telephones to complain that their delivery has not arrived at the correct time and they have been kept waiting for 2 hours.
- A customer returns an item of clothing, saying it is faulty, but you cannot see any sign of the fault.

Develop Your Skills

1. John Lewis has a famous policy that they call 'Never knowingly undersold'. Visit the John Lewis website and find out what this means for customers: www.johnlewis.com.

2. Marks and Spencer has a 35-day refund for all items purchased. Find out what this means for customers at www.marksandspencer.com.

Quick Test

1. Explain the drawbacks of offering guarantees to customers.

2. How can a business make sure that customers' complaints are handled correctly?

3. What should a business do if customers are constantly complaining?

Private sector businesses and public sector organisations

Private sector businesses

The main types of businesses in the private sector are:

- sole traders
- partnerships
- private limited companies

Sole traders

Sole traders are businesses that are owned and controlled by one individual. They provide the finance and run the business on a daily basis. They may employ other people, but basically the business belongs to them. Examples of sole traders include corner shops, hairdressers and painters.

Partnerships

A **partnership** is a business that is owned by between two and twenty partners. The partners provide the finance and run the business on a daily basis. Examples of partnerships include accountants, lawyers, doctors etc.

Both sole traders and partnerships have **unlimited liability**. This means that if the business fails then the owners must pay all the debts and liabilities – even to the point that their personal possessions (such as houses and cars) can be sold off.

Private limited company

A **private limited company** is owned by **shareholders**. The company name is usually followed by **Ltd**. The share ownership of the company is by invitation only and the shares are not sold on the stock exchange. Typically, private limited companies are owned by families and friends and they are run by a board of directors and managers. All the finance for the business comes from the shareholders but shareholders all have **limited liability**. This means that if the business fails then the shareholders can only lose the value of their investment in the company. Warburtons, IKEA and New Look are examples of well-known private limited companies.

EXAM TIP

It is important to know the difference between unlimited liability and limited liability.

The table below shows a useful comparison of these types of businesses in the private sector.

	Feature of Business			
	Ownership	**Finance**	**Control**	**Profits**
Sole trader	Sole trader	Provided by the sole trader	Sole trader	Sole trader
Partnership	2–20 partners	Provided by the partners but not always the same amount	Partners	Split amongst partners in an agreed ratio
Private limited company	Shareholders	Provided by the shareholders and limited	Board of Directors	Split amongst shareholders

Public sector organisations

Public Sector organisations are 'owned' by the public but are controlled by either local or central government. Local councils provide a range of services, such as education, recreation and leisure facilities, housing and social services. The finance for these services comes from central government taxes and local council taxes (council tax).

Apply Your Knowledge

Carry out a survey about the employers of people you know. Do they work for a sole trader, partnership, limited company or public sector organisation?

Develop Your Skills

Search businesses in your local area at www.yell.com/maps. You can enter the name of your home town and the type of business that you are looking for. For example, search for partnerships in Dundee, sole traders in Inverness, etc.

Quick Test

1. Explain the difference between limited and unlimited liability.
2. Describe the ownership of a private limited company.
3. Describe how profits are distributed in a partnership.

The third sector, charities and social enterprises

Third sector organisations

The **third sector** is made up of community groups, voluntary organisations, charities, social enterprises, co-operatives and individual volunteers. The third sector has an important contribution to make to the development of economic growth and to provide jobs and services for all aspects of the economy. Many of these groups and organisations do not aim to make a profit, instead they provide advice, support and education for a particular cause or charity. They raise funding from grants, donations, lottery etc.

The Scottish Council for Voluntary Organisations (SCVO) is the national body for Scotland's charities, voluntary organisations and social enterprises.

Charities

Charities exist for a variety of different causes. Charities aim to raise money to fund research for their particular cause or to help support those in need. Save the Children, Cancer Research and the RSPCA are examples of large well-known charities.

Social enterprises

Social enterprises are businesses that trade to tackle social problems and improve life for the community. They make their money from selling goods and services, but they reinvest a large portion of their profits back into the business or the local community. Social enterprises do not make profits for shareholders – because they do not have any. They do pay reasonable salaries to their employees and workers. Social enterprises are in our communities and on our high streets – from coffee shops and cinemas, to pubs and leisure centres, banks and bus companies. The Big Issue, Divine Chocolate and ASDAN are examples of well-known social enterprises.

Enterprise and organisations

All of the organisations and businesses in these two lessons on types of business organisation rely on their employees and workers having enterprising skills and attitudes. **Enterprise** is the idea behind a business or social enterprise. Enterprising skills and attitudes can be developed by everyone who works in a business or organisation.

An entrepreneur usually comes up with the original business idea, and uses their skills and abilities to turn the idea into a business reality. This involves not only taking risks and making important decisions, but also bringing together all the factors of production – land, labour and capital – in order for this to happen.

There are many famous entrepreneurs who have become millionaires, but many small social enterprises, community groups and voluntary organisations also have skilled entrepreneurs who keep these organisations running on a daily basis without becoming rich and famous.

Apply Your Knowledge

Find out about working as a volunteer in Scotland at www.volunteerscotland.org.uk. How do you think this differs from working in a business?

Develop Your Skills

Search third sector organisations in your local area at www.yell.com/maps. You can enter the name of your home town and the type of organisation that you are looking for. For example, search for social enterprises in Kirkcaldy, charities in Glasgow, etc.

Quick Test

1. What are the main aims of third sector organisations?
2. Explain why an entrepreneur might start-up a social enterprise business.

What are business objectives?

Objectives are goals or targets for the business to work towards. All businesses and organisations have **aims and objectives**; these are dependent on the type of business or organisation and also which sector of the economy they operate in.

Businesses and organisations may also have a **mission statement**, which usually sets out their strategic plans for the future. All objectives should contribute towards achieving the mission statement.

EXAM TIP

It is important to make a clear distinction between the objectives for the different sectors of the economy.

Private sector objectives

A major objective in the private sector (sole traders, partnerships, private limited companies) is **to make a profit**. However these businesses may also have other objectives, including:

- providing a good service or quality product for their customers
- surviving in the market
- growing the size of the business
- having a strong brand that customers will continue to buy
- being the market leader
- being socially responsible by caring for the environment and reducing waste

Public sector objectives

The main objective of organisations in the public sector is to **provide a service**. They use public funds from taxation to provide essential services at local and national level. In addition, they also aim to:

- meet the needs of local residents, for example by improving roads and providing leisure centres
- have a good reputation as a council or government
- cover their costs
- stick to their budget

Third sector objectives

The objectives of organisations in the third sector can vary. **Not-for-profit** organisations, such as community groups, volunteers and charities, have similar aims:

- help those in need of assistance
- help relieve poverty
- increase access to education
- increase donations and grants for their cause
- promote their message or cause

Social Enterprises that aim to make a **profit re-invest in the business** to keep people in jobs. Alternatively, the profits can be used to **improve the social community** in some way. In other words, they do not aim to make anyone rich.

Apply Your Knowledge

1. Research the aims and objectives of your local council. You should find these on your local council website.

2. Research the aims and objectives of your school. You should find these in the school handbook or from your school office.

Develop Your Skills

1. Divine Chocolate is a social enterprise. Find out about the stages of production – primary, secondary and tertiary – from the Divine Chocolate website (www.divinechocolate.com/about/bean-to-bar.aspx).

2. Oxfam is one of the largest charities in the UK. Visit the Oxfam website and find out the vision, values and goals of Oxfam.

Quick Test

1. Describe two objectives of a private sector business.
2. Describe the main objective of public sector organisations.
3. Describe two objectives of third sector organisations.
4. Describe how a social enterprise differs from a private limited company.

Factors that affect a business: 1

External factors

Businesses are affected by **external factors**. These are events and situations *outwith* the business that affect its performance overall. These factors can be positive or negative. Businesses have very little control over these factors.

Political 	The government can introduce laws that affect every business in the UK. Businesses have to comply with these laws and this usually costs them money. This in turn reduces their profits. Examples of such laws are the minimum wage, health and safety legislation and corporation tax.
Economic 	Economic factors refer to changes in the economy during periods of boom and slump. If there is a boom in the economy then businesses do well as they can charge high prices and make bigger profits. Customers will purchase more. However during a slump or a recession the opposite happens. Customers buy less as they cannot afford high prices. Businesses often cut their prices and this has a negative effect on their profits. Many businesses go bankrupt during a recession.
Social 	Social factors refer to the structure of the population overall. Businesses need to respond to the needs of the age and structure of the population but also to working patterns. Women make up a high percentage of the working population so this has seen an increase in child care provision. People are living longer, and therefore old people have needs and wants that have to be provided for. When the economy is doing well people want more luxury goods and holidays.
Technological 	Businesses must keep up with changes in technology. The introduction and availability of new technology will enable a business to produce new products and provide new services. The use of Internet and e-commerce has revolutionised shopping in the UK. Online retailers like eBay, Amazon and Argos have enabled customers to shop from the comfort of their own homes.

Environmental	All businesses face pressure (both socially and through government) to be environmentally friendly. They have to reduce waste and pollution. They also suffer from extremes of weather, such as floods, storms and extreme ice and snow. Often these weather conditions cause a drop in business trading and therefore a drop in profits.

Competition	All businesses face competition from other businesses in the UK and abroad. Competitors can attract customers by offering better products, services and prices. All businesses need to stay competitive by lowering prices and making sure that customers get the very best deal.

EXAM TIP

External factors are often referred to as **PESTEC**. This can help you to remember the headings easily.

Apply Your Knowledge

Outline the possible consequences to a business if the following external factors apply:
- competition attracts customers
- the Government changes the law regarding the minimum or living wage
- the economy is in recession

Develop Your Skills

The winters of 2010 and 2011 were particularly severe in Scotland, with heavy snowfalls and very low temperatures. Research the effect this had on Scottish businesses, especially in the period just before Christmas.

Quick Test

1. Describe how the government can affect the day-to-day running of a business.
2. Apart from bad weather, list the other environmental factors that can affect a business.

Factors that affect a business: 2

Internal factors

Businesses are affected by **internal factors**. These are events and situations *within* the business that affect its performance overall. These factors can be positive or negative and businesses have some degree of control over these factors.

Financial 	Businesses may not have enough finance to grow or expand. They may also experience periods where they have to cut costs by reducing services or products and making employees redundant. Wage rises and increases in the minimum wage or increases in the cost of raw materials and stocks can leave the businesses struggling to make profits. Alternatively, when finance is available the business can grow and employ more staff.
Human resources 	Well-trained staff are more productive in their work and help the business achieve its objectives. If staff are not trained and lack the required skills then this may lead to poor customer service and poor-quality products. Good managers motivate their staff to work hard and be successful but if managers are not properly skilled and trained, staff morale will decrease and the business will suffer. Businesses can also suffer if staff take industrial action.
Technological 	Changes in our modern society mean that businesses will fail if they do not use current technology and make sure that their staff are trained to maximise its use and efficiency. Technology is expensive to install and maintain, and breakdowns can be expensive. Technology on the production line includes machines, robots and equipment, and helps to produce good-quality products. Information technology, such as computers, mobile devices, smart phones and tablets, can change the way businesses operate and communicate with customers and employees.

Apply Your Knowledge

Outline the possible consequences to a business if the following internal factors apply:

- management are not trained properly to deal with employee weaknesses
- employees decide to take industrial action
- funding for new product development is difficult to source

Develop Your Skills

1. Research how cafes, restaurants and bars can take customer orders using hand-held devices which send the order to the main order desk via wireless network.

2. Research how online businesses such as Amazon and eBay can communicate with customers based on what they have previously purchased, for example the recommendations sent to customers by Amazon.

Quick Test

1. Explain the difference between internal and external factors.
2. Give the actions a business must take if it installs new technology.

Stakeholders: 1

What are the interests of stakeholders?

Stakeholders are individuals or groups of people who have both an **interest** in and an **influence** on a business. Stakeholders can be either internal of external.

Internal stakeholders are people who are *part of* your organisation, for example:

- owners (including shareholders)
- employees
- managers

External stakeholders are people *outwith* your organisation, for example:

- customers
- suppliers
- banks
- the Government
- the local community (including pressure groups)

The table below shows the main interests of stakeholders.

Stakeholder	Interest in the business
Owners/ Shareholders	They are interested in the profits the business makes, as this determines their share.
Employees	They are interested in the future of the business as they have a job they want to keep.
Managers	They are also interested in their jobs, salaries and bonuses.
Customers	They want value for money – good-quality products at good prices.
Suppliers	They want to provide goods to the business so that they will have continued custom and to ensure they get paid.
Banks	They are interested in the overall profitability of the business, which could be affected if they have provided loans to the business.

Stakeholder	Interest in the business
The Government	They want to make sure that the business pays taxes and obeys the law.
Local community	They want jobs for the local area but they also want their local community to be free from pollution and environmentally safe.

Apply Your Knowledge

1. Think of the stakeholders for your school. What influence can they have on your education?

2. Who are the stakeholders in your favourite football team? What interest do they have in the team?

Develop Your Skills

Local council planning committees have to deal with applications for new businesses on a regular basis. If you were a resident in the local community where a new factory is about to open, what would your arguments be both for and against this?

Quick Test

1. Name two internal and two external stakeholders.
2. What interest does the local community have in a business?
3. What interest does the Government have in a business?

Stakeholders: 2

What influence do stakeholders have on a business?

EXAM TIP

Stakeholders have both an interest in the business and an influence on the business.

Stakeholders can take actions that can positively or negatively affect the way the business operate.

Stakeholder	Influence on the business
Owners/ Shareholders	Owners make decisions that affect the business on a daily basis. Shareholders vote at the annual general meeting (AGM) to appoint directors and influence profit sharing.
Employees	Employees can choose to work hard and produce good-quality products and services. They can also take industrial action.
Managers	They make decisions every day that affect the business, for example new employees to hire, new products to develop, new procedures, etc.
Customers	They can choose to buy or not to buy products and pass on by word-of-mouth either their pleasure or displeasure.
Suppliers	They can provide good-quality raw materials at reasonable prices. However they can also provide poor-quality products and they can increase their prices.
Banks	They can refuse to provide finance, which may put the business in a difficult position.
Local community	They can complain to the local council about the actions of a business.
The Government	The government can pass laws at any time, and the business has to comply with these laws.

Apply Your Knowledge

1. Who are Tesco's main stakeholders? What interest do they have over the business?

2. Who are the main stakeholders for your favourite band? What influence do they have over them?

Develop Your Skills

The Government regularly reviews the minimum wage paid to employees. Find out what the current minimum wage is and what age groups it applies to.

Quick Test

1. Outline actions that employees can take which may affect the business.

2. Describe the consequences for a business if they have to change supplier.

3. Describe the main actions that customers can take if they are not happy with a business.

Recruitment

Recruitment is the process of getting potential candidates to apply for a job vacancy.

Recruitment methods

Recruitment can be conducted **internally** or **externally**. With internal recruitment, job vacancies are filled by existing staff. The jobs may be advertised internally and all interested candidates can apply and be interviewed if they are suitable. The jobs may also be filled by promoting employees – perhaps after appraisal interviews.

With external recruitment, a vacancy is filled by open competition and advertisement. Exisiting employees will be allowed to apply but applications are invited from outwith the organisiation.

Stages of the recruitment process

Each business or organisation will go through a number of stages in order to recruit the best employee.

Identifying the job vacancy
This simply means making sure that the job actually exists and the reasons why.

Conducting a job analysis
This involves identifying in more detail what the role actually involves. What are the tasks and duties that will be carried out in the job?

Preparing a job description
A job description is a detailed account of the job. This is usually sent to applicants for the post to help identify if this is a suitable job for them. The job description will include: the job title, the duties and responsibilities, the location of the job, the salary, the working conditions and holidays and any benefits, for example pension arrangements.

Preparing a person specification
A person specification is also prepared after the job analysis has been done. It outlines details of the type of person the business is looking for to do the job. The person specification will include essential and desirable attributes: **essential** means the applicant must have them and **desirable** means it would be better if they have them. The person specification might ask for: skills, qualities, qualifications, experience and any additional requirements, such as a driving licence.

> **EXAM TIP**
>
> It is important to know the difference between a job description, which is about the job itself, and a person specification, which is about the type of person the business is looking for to fill the job.

Advertising the vacancy internally and externally

Job vacancies can be advertised in a variety of different ways and places, such as newspapers, magazines, on Internet websites, in job centres etc.

Alternatively the business may ask a **recruitment agency** to find them a suitable candidate. The agency will take responsibility for advertising the job, right through to interviewing the candidates. This is very useful if the business is very small and does not have the expertise for recruiting. However large businesses also use agencies as it is less time-consuming for them.

Application forms and CVs

Sending out application forms is straightforward. Each applicant can be sent out a form or alternatively they can complete an online application form. Application forms are useful because the business receives the same information in the same format from each candidate.

Businesses may ask candidates to send in their CV rather than complete an application form. This is a summary of the candidate's skills, abilities, experience and qualifications. It is designed by the candidate and a good CV can show off their talents in the best possible light.

Businesses may also ask candidates to send in a reference from their current or past employer. The reference should outline the skills of the candidate and their performance in their current or past job.

Apply Your Knowledge

Describe the benefits to a business of candidates completing online application forms and the advantages to candidates of sending in a CV.

Develop Your Skills

Visit www.s1jobs.com to see the wide variety of jobs that are advertised across Scotland on a daily basis. What information do employers give?

Quick Test

1. Compare internal and external recruitment.
2. Identify three pieces of information contained in a job description.
3. Describe what a recruitment agency would use a person specification for.
4. Identify three places where jobs can be advertised externally.

Selection of employees

The selection process

Once all the applications and CVs have been received from candidates, the selection process begins to find the best person to fill the job vacancy.

There are many different methods of selection. Firstly, the business should compare the candidates with the person specification to see if they meet the criteria. Those who do meet the criteria are invited to take part in one of many different selection methods. The selection process may take place at the business itself or they may use an assessment centre, which could be based at a recruitment agency.

EXAM TIP

It is important that businesses match the candidates' applications with the person specification otherwise they will find it difficult to reject applications.

Selection methods

The interview

Before the interview the business should decide on an interview panel, plus where and when the interviews will take place. Most importantly, they have to prepare suitable questions to ask the candidates.

During the interview the panel will make notes on what each candidate says, so that afterwards they can compare answers from all the candidates.

In order to assist with the selection, the panel should also consider references from previous employers. References or referees provide a report on the applicant to back up their application. This will normally state how reliable, honest and suitable the candidate is for the job.

Once the final decision has been made, the successful candidate will be offered the job and they will arrange how and when to start work.

Giving a presentation

Candidates may be asked to give a presentation to the panel. This could involve using a flip chart, or a computer and data projector.

Role play

Candidates may be asked to take part in a scenario that shows how they react in different situations, such as dealing with a difficult customer. The role play is designed to show the strengths, weaknesses and personality of the candidates.

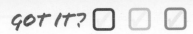
Group interviews or discussions

Candidates may be asked to take part in a discussion with all the other short-listed candidates. This should show who emerges as natural leaders and what type of interpersonal skills the candidates have.

Team-building tasks

Candidates may be asked to work as part of a team to solve a particular problem. They would be expected to work together to come up with an acceptable solution. Again, this tests the candidates' interpersonal skills.

Personality or aptitude tests

These are usually done alongside another form of selection. For example the candidate may sit the test at the end of their interview. The idea behind these tests is simply to find out the knowledge, ability and personality of the candidates. Many of these tests are now done online.

Apply Your Knowledge

1. What information would a business need to give to an assessment centre before they carried out selection tests on applicants for a job?

2. Prepare three interview questions for the post of Customer Service Manager.

3. Can you accurately assess a candidate who has kept quiet during a group discussion?

Develop Your Skills

1. What would you include in a team-building task for the post of Marketing Assistant?

2. How important is the appearance of the candidate at an interview?

3. What leadership skills are employers looking for in a group discussion task?

Quick Test

1. Give the advantages of using an interview as the only means of selecting a candidate for a job.

2. Describe the disadvantages of using personality tests as a means of selecting candidates.

3. Describe the role an assessment centre plays in the recruitment process.

Training of employees

Types of training

- **On-the-job training** is carried out in the work place. It is undertaken by employees to improve their knowledge, skills and performance at work.
- **Off-the-job training** is carried out away from the work place. It can be undertaken at college, university, training centre or other venue. It may involve additional qualifications. The training is usually delivered by experts in their field.
- **Induction training** is usually carried out in the work place. It is offered to new employees and can include training about the wider business environment as well as specific training about the new job. Induction training usually also involves health and safety issues, arrangements for signing in and out, holidays, sickness, social arrangements etc.

Methods of training

Whichever type of training is undertaken, it can be done in a variety of ways to suit the business, the employees or the product or service of the organisation.

- **Lectures** are often used for off-the-job training to reach large numbers of people at once. They are a useful way of giving information.
- **Role playing and simulation** enable employees to react in a realistic way to solving customer problems or dealing with other colleagues. Employees are asked to 'play out' a scenario and to learn from this.
- **Job rotation** involves moving an employee through a series of jobs so they can get a good feel for the tasks that are associated with different roles.
- **Apprenticeships** are especially appropriate for jobs requiring production skills, for example plumbing, engineering etc. However, they are also used now for administration and business jobs for young employees.
- **Multimedia** training can take a variety of different forms, such as DVDs, PowerPoint presentations, films, computer simulations, etc. Many of these can be undertaken by the employee in their own time away from work.

Costs and benefits of training

Training employees is expensive, therefore businesses have to weigh up the costs and benefits in order to make sure it is worthwhile.

Type of Training	Costs	Benefits
On-the-job	• Time can be lost to do the employee's job. • Employees may feel awkward being trained by each other.	• Training is specific to the job. • No time is lost away from the work place.
Off-the-job	• Time is spent away from the work place. • The cost of paying for training and qualifications can be high.	• Training can be done by experts so the quality is high. • Employees can be highly motivated to receive additional qualifications.

Apply Your Knowledge

1. What elements would you include in an induction training programme for a new teacher at your school?

2. What training or teaching methods do you experience at school each day? Which of these do you enjoy the most?

Develop Your Skills

How would you persuade an employee to undertake a training programme that took them 'off-the-job'?

Quick Test

1. Explain the difference between on-the-job and off-the-job training.
2. Describe two costs and two benefits of on-the-job training.
3. Describe two methods of employee training that could be run off-the-job.
4. Describe what induction training is.

Motivating and retaining employees

Motivating staff

Employers want to keep their employees happy. If employees are happy they are more likely to do a good job and stay with the business.

Financial rewards

Methods of payment to employees are varied. The main ones are outlined below.

- **Time rates** – Employees are paid by the hour. The government has set a minimum hourly wage, which must be paid to all employees. However different jobs will pay different rates per hour.

- **Piece rates** – Employees are paid according to the amount they produce. This has to be measured in some way. If employees work harder and produce more, they can earn more.

- **Wage/salary (flat rate)** – Employees are paid an agreed wage or salary per week or per month for doing their job. The wage or salary does not usually change and is not related to the amount they produce or sell.

- **Overtime** – Hours worked beyond the normal working day or week. Overtime is often paid at 1.5 times or double the employee's normal rate.

- **Bonus** – Bonuses are paid over and above the normal wage or salary for a variety of reasons. For example, meeting a target or producing the most.

Non-financial rewards

These are other ways of rewarding staff, which do not involve direct payments. They are often called 'perks'.

- **Company Car** – The business pays for a car for the employee to use.

- **Pension/Insurance** – All employers now have to contribute to pension funds for their employees' retirement. Many also pay medical insurance or life insurance for their employees.

- **Luncheon vouchers/subsidised canteen/staff discount** – Some employers will pay for lunches or provide canteen facilities where employees can buy meals at reduced prices. Many large retail companies also offer their staff a discount.

- **Childcare vouchers/crèche schemes** – Some employers allow their employees to claim childcare vouchers to pay for childcare while they are at work. Others provide a crèche within the building for employee's children.

EXAM TIP

Employees choose an employer for a variety of reasons – not just the salary. So additional benefits such as rewards are important in attracting the right candidates to the job.

Employee relations

Businesses try and keep their employees motivated in other ways too: team working, good holiday arrangements, staff training, appraisal systems and involving employees in meetings and decision-making will all help to motivate staff. Other businesses go further:

- **Works council** – A committee made up of employees and managers, which enables the employees to be consulted and involved in the decision-making process of the business.
- **Quality circles** – Groups of volunteer employees who meet to discuss issues for improvement in the business. They focus on production, training and customer service.
- **Employee of the month and achievement awards** – Many businesses operate schemes whereby employees can receive awards, bonuses or recognition for their role in the business.
- **The working environment** – Many businesses have provided rooms for relaxation or playing games. Some offer reduced price or free gym membership.

Apply Your Knowledge

Describe how winning an achievement award at school or college would make you feel. List the ways it would make you work harder afterwards.

Develop Your Skills

You are the Human Resources Manager in a large company. Your employees have completed a survey that shows they are not happy at work. Describe how you plan to try and change that.

Quick Test

1. Explain what 'double time' is when paying employees.
2. Define the phrase 'non-financial rewards'.
3. Give two examples of non-financial rewards.
4. Describe the role of a works council.

Trade unions

Trade unions

A trade union is an organisation that employees can join to help them negotiate better pay and conditions. It will advise union members and help resolve disputes with employers and may also offer additional benefits to its employees such as financial services and legal advice.

Industrial Action

When no agreement can be reached between the employer and trade unions industrial action can occur. There are different methods of industrial action – some more damaging than others. All forms of industrial action penalise the business but employees can also suffer.

- **Strike** – Employees refuse to go to work but do not get paid.
- **Overtime ban** – Employees refuse to work overtime and lose pay.
- **Sit-in** – Employees occupy the premises and normal work cannot take place.
- **Work to rule** – Employees only do exactly what their contract states. Goodwill is lost and some overtime payments may be lost.
- **Go slow** – Employees still carry out their duties but do so more slowly or with reduced productivity.

No matter what method of action the employee takes, they will lose their wage or salary for the time that they are not working.

There can be positive benefits from industrial action, for example new procedures can be introduced that all employees will follow and be happy with.

Apply Your Knowledge

Explain whether you think strikes work. If employees go on strike they will lose pay – the employer may be happy about that. But what about the customers of the business? Describe who you think wins or loses when employees go on strike.

Develop Your Skills

Learn more about Trade Unions by going to http://www.tuc.org.uk. This is the website of the Trade Union Congress in the UK and has lots of information about joining a Trade Union and about employees' rights at work.

Quick Test

1. What is a trade union and what does it do?
2. Why does industrial action sometimes take place?
3. What is the difference between a strike and a sit-in?

Legislation

Legislation

EXAM TIP

You are not expected to know these laws in detail but you are expected to have a basic understanding of what the law is trying to do.

There are a number of laws that have to be followed by both employers and employees. The laws are designed to make the working environment safe and to ensure that employees are treated fairly in the work place.

Health and Safety at Work Act 1974

This law outlines the responsibilities of both employers and employees in relation to health and safety at work. Employers have a duty to:

- provide and maintain safety equipment and safe systems of work
- ensure materials used are properly stored, handled, used and transported
- provide information, training, instruction and supervision
- provide a safe place of employment, e.g. fire extinguishers, protective clothing
- have health and safety representatives

Employees have a duty to:

- take reasonable care of the health and safety of themselves and of others who may be affected by what they do or do not do
- co-operate with the employer on health and safety matters

The Equality Act 2010

The Equality Act 2010 bans unfair treatment and helps achieve equal opportunities in the workplace and in wider society. It brings together previous acts that deal with discrimination and makes it unlawful to discriminate against anyone on the grounds of:

- sex
- race
- marital status
- religion and belief
- disability
- sexual orientation
- pregnancy

Any employee who feels that they have been discriminated against under any of these categories may have a case against their employer.

The Freedom of Information Act 2000

This Act allows the general public access to information held by public bodies such as the government and local authorities. It is designed to build trust in the government as the public know that they can ask for information at any time.

Information can come from schools, hospitals, the police, local council and other public bodies.

The Data Protection Act 1998

The Data Protection Act 1998 allows individuals to have access to information about themselves. Any company or organisation that wants to hold data must apply to the Data Protection Registrar. The data must be held according to certain principles, for example it must be accurate and up-to-date, it must be obtained fairly and lawfully and it must be protected against misuse.

The Minimum Wage Act 1998

This law was passed to ensure that employees received a minimum wage in order to avoid poverty and exploitation. The minimum wage varies depending on the age of the employee. The rate is set by the government and increases are applied each year.

Apply Your Knowledge

Why do you think employees could be discriminated against in the workplace? Explain your reasons.

Develop Your Skills

Log onto www.hse.gov.uk and find the current statistics for accidents and days lost from work.

Quick Test

1. Describe the duties of employees under the Health and Safety at Work Act.
2. Explain two ways that employees may be discriminated against at work.
3. Describe two features of the Data Protection Act.

Sources of finance: 1

Sources of finance for the private sector

Businesses need finance to start-up and to keep going. There is a range of sources of finance that are suitable for different purposes.

Source of finance	Description	Suitable for...
Loan from family and friends	Family and friends may provide a business with finance and often this does not need to be paid back.	Sole trader Partnership
Capital from owners	The owners provide their own finance, e.g. from savings or redundancy payments.	Sole trader Partnership Private limited company
Bank loan	Finance can be borrowed from a bank and repaid with interest. The payments are agreed for a fixed period.	Sole trader Partnership Private limited company
Bank overdraft	The bank allows the business to take more out of the account than is in it – i.e. a negative balance.	Sole trader Partnership Private limited company (for short periods of time)
Government grants	Finance can be obtained from the government if the business meets certain criteria. Grants usually do not have to be repaid.	Sole trader Partnership Private limited company
Prince's Trust	The Prince's Trust will provide start-up capital for young entrepreneurs.	Sole trader
Shares	The business can issues more shares to shareholders in order to raise more finance.	Private limited company
Mortgage	This can be obtained from a bank or building society and is usually used to buy property over a long period of time.	Sole trader Partnership Private limited company

Source of finance	Description	Suitable for...
Hire purchase	This can be used to obtain equipment and machinery. Payments are made over an agreed period of time but the equipment does not belong to the business until the final payment is made.	Sole trader Partnership Private limited company

EXAM TIP

Not all businesses are financed in the same way. It depends on how much finance they need and for how long.

Apply Your Knowledge

If you were starting up in business as a sole trader what would be your preferred sources of finance? Give reasons for your choice.

Develop Your Skills

Log onto www.scottishenterprise.com to find out how businesses in Scotland can obtain funding.

Quick Test

1. Name three sources of finance for a sole trader.
2. Explain what a bank overdraft is.
3. Describe what a mortgage is usually given for.

Sources of finance: 2

Sources of finance for the public sector

Public sector organisations obtain their finance in a different way. The government collects income tax and other forms of taxation throughout the year, for example road tax, corporation tax and VAT. The government then distributes this income according to their spending plans and will allocate a certain amount to the NHS, transport, industry etc. In Scotland funding for some services (such as education) comes from the Scottish Parliament.

Sources of finance for the third sector

Third sector finance is not fixed, and will change depending on how the economy is performing and how much grant funding is available from the government and other sources, such as European funding.

Type of finance	Source
Gift finance	Individuals, businesses, sponsorship, the lottery, legacies, fundraising etc.
Grant funding	Government, local authority, enterprise companies, Prince's Trust, European Union.
Trading activities	Charity shops, social enterprises, cafes.

Apply Your Knowledge

Find out why the government gives grants to businesses in certain areas of the country.

Develop Your Skills

Find out more about the way in which the UK Government spends income from taxation at www.publicspending.co.uk. Here you can see a breakdown of the amount spent on different areas of the economy.

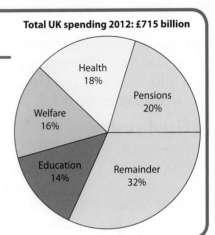

Total UK spending 2012: £715 billion

Health 18%

Pensions 20%

Welfare 16%

Education 14%

Remainder 32%

Quick Test

1. How does the government obtain finance for spending on the economy?

2. What is VAT?

3. Identify one method of obtaining finance in the third sector.

Costs and the break even point

Types of cost

Costs are the bills that businesses need to pay on a regular basis. Some of these costs change regularly whilst others do not change regularly. These costs are explained below.

Fixed costs

Fixed costs are the bills or expenses that the business has to pay that **do not change** according to output. The important point to remember about fixed costs is that they always have to be paid. Examples of fixed costs are: rent of factory, manager's salary, council tax, rates.

Variable costs

Variable costs are the business's bills and expenses **that do change** according to output. The more the business produces the higher the variable costs are going to be. Variable costs are the cost of materials for the product, the cost of labour, etc. Examples of variable costs are: raw materials, wages, electricity, gas.

Total costs

For a business, the total cost of production is the fixed costs plus the variable costs. Once all these costs have been calculated the business can then start to work out the profit or loss.

EXAM TIP

Fixed costs do not change as output changes. They always have to be paid.

EXAM TIP

Variable costs rise or fall according to output.

EXAM TIP

Total costs = fixed costs + variable costs.

Break even point

The **break even point** is the point that sales revenue and total costs are equal and the business is not making either a profit or a loss.

Calculating profit

Profits are made just above the break even point. This is the point at which sales revenue is higher than total costs.

Break even graph

The break even point can be shown very clearly on a graph. This is a useful tool for analysing sales and costs.

TR = total revenue, TC = total costs, FC = fixed costs. The break even point is where the TR and TC lines cross.

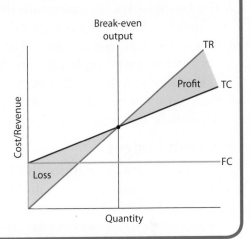

Apply Your Knowledge

Businesses that are just starting up often forget about their fixed costs. What do you think businesses should do to make sure that they cover their fixed costs?

Develop Your Skills

The break even point can be calculated easily using a spreadsheet. Find out how to enter figures into a spreadsheet to calculate the break even point.

Quick Test

1. Describe fixed costs.
2. Describe variable costs.
3. Give one example of a fixed cost and one example of a variable cost.
4. Explain the break even point.

Cash budgeting

Cash flow

The business has to make sure that it has enough cash coming in on a regular basis in order to be able to pay its bills on time. This overall concept is called **cash flow**. A business has to make sure that its cash flow is good, otherwise it risks going into liquidation (or going bankrupt). Many businesses fail because they run short of cash. They may have allowed too many customers a long credit period, but in the meantime the business has to pay its own bills. Businesses must anticipate periods when they may run short of cash and take action to deal with this.

A cash budget

This is a financial plan for the future, for example 3–6 months ahead. A cash budget identifies the expected bills and expenses for the business and the projected revenue or income from sales. A simple cash budget is shown below.

Rosco Ltd Cash Budget	Jan (£)	Feb (£)	Mar (£)
Opening Balance	1000	2900	2000
Cash In			
Sales	13000	9000	8000
Total In	*14000*	*11900*	*10000*
Cash Out			
Purchases of stock	9000	8000	8500
Wages	1000	1000	1000
Electricity	600	500	450
Gas	500	400	400
Total Out	*11100*	*9900*	*10350*
Closing Balance	**2900**	**2000**	**−350**

The closing balance is £-350 in March. It is a projection into the future, but we can see that this *will* happen if the business owner does not take some action.

Cash flow problems and how to solve them

The cash budget will let the owner/s of a business see what problems they may have in the future regarding cash flow. Cash flow problems can be solved by doing some or all of the following: obtaining a loan or overdraft from the bank; raising extra capital; cutting back on projected expenses; asking suppliers or creditors for extra time to pay bills; spreading the cost of assets, for example hire purchase or leasing; cutting down on purchases of stock, e.g. finding a cheaper supplier; encouraging customer to pay on time, for example by offering discounts.

Generating and spending cash

Businesses generate **cash** by selling goods and services. Payments are received from customers in the form of cash, cheques, credit card payments or bank transfers. This is often referred to as 'cash in' or 'money in'. Some sales to customers are made on a **credit** basis. This means that the customers receive the goods immediately but that payment follows approximately 1 month later.

All businesses have bills to pay. They have to pay for the raw materials or goods that they are going to sell to their customers. This is normally referred to as stock. In addition they have to pay day-to-day bills such as electricity, gas, insurance, wages, petrol, telephone etc. This is often referred to as 'cash out' or 'money out'. Some suppliers allow the business 1 month to pay their bills.

Apply Your Knowledge

1. What are the main causes of cash flow problems in a business?

2. Why is it necessary to prepare a cash budget?

Develop Your Skills

Enter the figures from the cash budget section into a spreadsheet and use the formula function to work out the closing balances. Now change some of the figures for expenses and sales and see how quickly and easily the closing balance figures change.

Quick Test

1. Give two advantages of preparing a cash budget.
2. Identify two expenses for a business.
3. Describe two ways in which a business could solve cash flow problems.
4. Explain how a spreadsheet can help to improve cash flow.

Profit statement

Trading and profit and loss account

All businesses have to prepare statements to show how much profit or loss they are making. This will differ in complexity for different types of businesses, but the most common statement is a **trading and profit and loss account**. This is prepared by a business that buys-in finished products and sells them again in order to make a profit.

The trading and profit and loss account shows the gross and net profits made by the business. Gross profit is the profit made from buying and selling. Net profit is the profit made after all the expenses of the business have been deducted. An example is shown below.

Trading and profit and loss account for Rosco Ltd, year ending 31 December		
	£000	£000
Sales		300
Less cost of sales		
Opening stock	20	
Add purchases	110	
	130	
Less closing Stock	20	
Cost of goods sold		110
Gross profit		**190**
Less Expenses		
Wages	25	
Electricity	10	
Gas	10	
		45
Net profit		**145**

> **EXAM TIP**
>
> Gross profit is made from buying and selling finished goods. Net profit is made after all the expenses of the business have been deducted.

The business must be able to identify the reasons for profits and losses. In the statement above the business has made a net profit of £145,000. However, if expenses rise or sales fall this profit will be reduced. In this case does the business have to reduce unnecessary expenses or do they have to increase the selling price of their products? There may be more than one solution to the problem.

Production costs

A business that manufactures or produces products and then sells them will require a different type of profit statement. They will produce a statement that shows how much it has actually cost to manufacture the products and then sell them as finished goods. Production costs include the following:

- the cost of buying raw materials
- the cost of labour to make the raw materials into finished goods

Overhead production costs

There are other costs associated with running the factory where production takes place. These are known as overheads and include:

- electricity, gas and insurance
- managers salaries
- costs of supplies, for example cleaning products

Apply Your Knowledge

How do businesses increase their profits? They have bills to pay but cannot always rely on sales increasing. How do they survive when business conditions are difficult?

Develop Your Skills

Enter the figures above from the trading and profit and loss account into a spreadsheet. Insert formulas at the appropriate places. Change some of the expenses and see how gross and net profit figures change.

Quick Test

1. Describe what gross profit is.
2. Describe what net profit is.
3. Give two production costs.
4. List two overhead costs.

New technology: 1

Spreadsheets

The finance function in a business can be enhanced through the use of spreadsheets and other accounting packages. Spreadsheets and databases can be used to set up and produce customer invoices using a mail merge function. The software performs all the calculations and records outstanding balances. Calculations are accurate and very quick. Accounting packages can produce profit statements that allow the business to manage their financial performance. Spreadsheets can be used to prepare cash budgets and manage cash flow. Thus business managers can quickly answer the following questions.

- Which customers still have outstanding bills and how much are they?

- How much cash is in the bank?

- What was the profit last year compared to this year?

- What is the total of the business costs or expenses, and where do they need to cut down?

Electronic training resources

Both existing and new employees require ongoing training. Many organisations have now developed electronic training resources for this. Examples include:

- online videos
- E-learning courses that test at each stage of training and interactive resources that give feedback
- DVDs

These electronic resources allow flexibility for the employee to learn at a time and place of their own choosing. They also reduce the amount of time spent away from the work place and allow employers to provide good-quality training at a reduced cost.

Employee records

Database management systems allow employers to hold up-to-date records about their employees and their service history. All personal details can be held in a database along with training details, salary, promotions and other information that can enhance an employee's overall profile in the organisation.

Apply Your Knowledge

Why would a business manager use a spreadsheet? How could a spreadsheet be used to prepare a Cash Budget? Think about the formula you would need to calculate the closing balance each month.

Develop Your Skills

Find out more about online learning. Two very famous organizations in the UK have online learning sites for both business and leisure. Go to http://www.bbc.co.uk/learning and http://www.channel4learning.com to have a look at the full range of courses, topics and subjects that can be studied or accessed online.

Quick Test

1. Describe two ways that spreadsheets can be used to help business managers.
2. List two ways that businesses can use technology to train employees.

New technology: 2

Psychometric electronic testing

Many businesses now ask potential employees to complete online aptitude tests or personality tests, often called psychometric tests. The candidate will be given details of the website to log onto and complete a series of tests or questions. The results are analysed and the employer can then choose who to interview on the basis of the test results. This can save huge amounts of time as candidates who are not suitable do not have to be called for interview.

Psychometric tests can be adapted to suit the requirements of the employer. For example the police, army and navy will have quite different tests than childcare providers or engineering companies.

Recruitment and electronic application forms

Employers now use websites to advertise job vacancies and manage the recruitment process. The main recruitment websites are used by hundreds of thousands of candidates and employers each day. In Scotland some of the most popular websites are:

- www.s1jobs.com
- www.myjobscotland.gov.uk
- www.scotcareers.co.uk
- www.monster.co.uk
- www.scottishjobs.com

All of these websites allow the applicants to set up their own account and store their personal details and CV. This means that they do not have to re-enter the same information each time they want to apply for a job. The websites carry hundreds of job vacancies and will email candidates when jobs are advertised that suit their profile. Many of the websites offer advice on interview techniques and completing job applications.

Candidates apply online for their chosen job. They may have to complete a standard application form or they can email their CV to the potential employer. All interviews are usually arranged by email.

Apply Your Knowledge

1. Prepare your own CV by using the suggested headings in the job websites listed above.

2. What do you think are the main skills that employers are looking for in young people?

Develop Your Skills

1. Log onto the recruitment websites listed above and search for jobs in your local area or a location that interests you. Read the information provided about the jobs.

2. Log onto any website that carries out psychometric tests. Test yourself to see what type of career you might be suited to.

Quick Test

1. Explain how online testing can save time for employers recruiting candidates.
2. Describe the advantages to employers of online applications.

Who are your customers?

Every business needs customers, as without them buying goods and services, the business will fail. Customers have a wide variety of choice and will return to the businesses that they are happy with both in terms of the product or service and the customer service they experience. Businesses have to know who their customers are, and what their customers want. This can be done through market research and marketing activities.

Market segments

Businesses must know who their customers are and what their customers' needs are. Many products fail because the correct customers were not targeted. Customers are usually segmented into different groups based on certain factors.

Age	Products can be aimed at different age groups, for example young children age 0–5 years, teenagers age 13–17 years, or older people age 50+ years (Saga Holidays are aimed at people over 50).
Gender	Males and females are targeted with different products. For example, makeup is mostly aimed at women while aftershave is aimed at men.
Income	Luxury products like yachts, cruises and expensive jewellery are aimed at people with high incomes. People with low incomes are targeted by cheaper supermarkets, such as Aldi and Lidl.
Social class	Some products are targeted according to social class, for example home furnishings, or leisure activities such as skiing.

There are other factors that can be taken into account when targeting customers, such as geographical location. For example, people living in hot countries need different clothes from those living in cold countries.

By concentrating on market segments, businesses can:

- adjust their products to specific requirements
- set the price to reflect the target customers, for example low prices or high prices
- design advertising that targets the particular market segment
- decide where to sell their products in order to reach these customers

This is known as target marketing.

EXAM TIP

Carrying out market research is fairly straightforward. However the analysis of the information, and then acting on the results, is more difficult and costs businesses money.

Apply Your Knowledge

- Does everyone clearly fit into a market segment category?
- Do all teenagers want the same products?
- Do all people over 50 years of age want to go on a Saga Holiday?

Thinking about the answers to these questions should lead you to the view that market segmentation is not an exact science. People do not all fit neatly into a segment. Some people cross over many different segments. However, market segmentation is a useful tool for marketing purposes.

Quick Test

1. Explain why businesses need to know who their customers are
2. What is meant by market segments?
3. Why is it important to target specific market segments?
4. What products would you aim at children aged 5–8 years?

Market research: 1

What is market research?

Market research is the name given to the process whereby businesses find out information about their customers and about the market. Market research involves finding out what customers want, but also finding out about what other businesses are selling and for how much. Once this information has been gathered, it is analysed and decisions are made about what actions the business should take.

Some of the decisions could include:

- altering the price of the product
- changing the product in some way
- launching a new product onto the market
- changing where the product is sold

There are two main methods of market research. They are called field research and desk research.

We will look at field research here and at desk research on page 64.

Field research

Field research involves going out into the market place and finding out information for your own business. This is called primary information.

Methods

Questionnaire and/or survey	This can be done in different ways, but in general you ask people their opinions or their ideas. The main point is that you are asking about your own specific product.
Consumer panel	A group of customers can be brought together to discuss a product or compare it to other products. Their opinions and ideas are noted down at the time.

| Hall test | This involves giving a free sample or trial of a product to a group of customers and they are asked to give their opinion once they have tried it out. |
| Observation | A lot of information can be gathered by observing customers. Observation could take place in a shop, or in the high street. Behaviours can then be analysed. |

Costs and benefits of field research

Costs of Field Research	Benefits of Field Research
Very expensive to carry out	The information gathered is relevant.
Very time-consuming	The information is accurate as it is first hand.

EXAM TIP

Field research is extremely important for finding out customers' opinions. However, what the business then does with the information is also very important.

Apply Your Knowledge

- How would you undertake a survey of pupils in your class?
- Would you ask questions of each person individually?
- Can you think of different ways to carry out your survey?
- How could you use ICT to help you with your survey?

Develop Your Skills

Use the Survey Monkey website (www.surveymonkey.com) to create a short survey for students in your class about their favourite ice-cream.

Use the 'sign up free for just the basics' option.

Quick Test

1. Explain what is meant by market research.
2. How does market research help a business?
3. Why would a researcher carry out an interview instead of a postal survey?
4. What is the main benefit of field research?

Market research: 2

Here we look at the second method of market research: desk research.

Desk research

Desk research involves finding out information from existing sources, using information that has already been gathered by other businesses or organisations, in order to help your business. This is called secondary information.

Methods

Government data	The government publishes information from a variety of sources, for example the Census or the Family Expenditure Survey.

Printed media	These contain information from a variety of sources about consumer behaviour and spending patterns. Examples of printed media include books, journals, magazines and newspapers.

Online research	There is a vast amount of data available from business websites, which can be used for market research purposes. For example, the Chamber of Commerce provides information about businesses and new opportunities.

Costs and Benefits of Desk Research

Costs of Desk Research	Benefits of Desk Research
The information may not be relevant to your business.	The information does not always cost money to obtain
The information may not always be accurate.	Very often the information is free and is relatively easy to obtain.

Apply Your Knowledge

1. The government conducts a census every 10 years in the UK. How can businesses make use of this information?

2. How do you know which sources of information to trust online?

Develop Your Skills

Access the Scotland's Census 2011 website: http://www.scotlandscensus.gov.uk
Read the section called 'How census data shapes our future'.

Quick Test

1. What is desk research?
2. Outline two methods of desk research.
3. What is the main benefit of desk research?

The marketing mix: 1

The **marketing mix** is often referred to as the **4Ps** – product, price, promotion and place. Each of the 4Ps is unique in its own way but the combination of the 4Ps allows a business to develop a marketing strategy that works and enables products and services to be sold and therefore profits made.

This chapter describes the first element of the marketing mix: product.

Product

This is the product or service that is being sold by the business. The product should have been developed in such a way that the business is confident that it will sell.

Products are launched onto the market after a careful development process.

1. An idea is generated.

2. Market research is undertaken.

3. Product research is undertaken.

4. A prototype is developed.

5. The prototype is tested on the market.

6. Adaptations are made on the basis of market testing.

7. The product is launched.

It can take several years to complete all of these stages. However, once a product is launched onto the market it follows a natural product life cycle.

The product life cycle

Most products go through a recognised cycle during their life. The product life can be short or long but the stages are the same. The stages of the product life cycle are shown below.

Introduction: the product is introduced or launched onto the market.

Growth: once customers know about the product, sales begin to grow.

Maturity: at this stage everyone who wants the product has already purchased it, and sales level out.

Decline: sales of the product start to fall as there are no new customers.

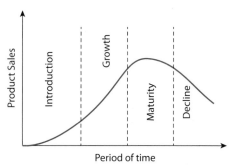

A business can inject new life into a product to try and prolong the life cycle. This can be done by altering any element of the marketing mix, i.e. the product itself, the price, the place where it is sold or how it is promoted.

Product branding

A product that is a 'brand name' is easily identified and attracts loyal customers. A brand can be a single product or a group of products from the same company, for example Ford, Cadbury and Campbell's all sell many products under the same company name. Branding products in this way encourages customers to keep coming back as they know they will buy a good product with an accepted level of quality. Branded products usually have an easily identifiable logo and a slogan; and customers are often prepared to pay more if they associate the brand with prestige (for example they will pay more for a designer t-shirt). Branded products usually allow the business to make profits quite easily.

Apply Your Knowledge

Find out how some famous brands have prolonged the life cycle of their products by making changes, for example Polo, Kit Kats, Crème Eggs.

Develop Your Skills

Go to BBC Bitesize revision website and choose Business Studies/Marketing to find out more about the marketing mix.

Quick Test

1.   Describe three stages of the product development process.
2.   Name the four stages of the product life cycle.
3.   Suggest two ways that the product life cycle can be extended.

The marketing mix: 2

This chapter explores the second and third elements of the marketing mix – price and promotion.

Price

The price of any product is important and sensitive to the demands of the market. There are a number of factors to be considered when setting prices for a product.

- What did it cost to make?
- What price are competitors charging?
- Is the product sensitive to very small changes in price?

Businesses usually adopt a pricing strategy based on the above factors. The most common pricing strategies are:

- **High price** – Setting a higher price for the product than competitors because the business is confident that consumers will pay it.
- **Low price** – Setting a lower price for the product to try and undercut the competition.
- **Cost plus pricing** – Based on the cost of producing the product. The manufacturer then decides on how much they want to make in terms of profit and add this on, usually as a percentage of the cost.
- **Penetration pricing** – Setting the price low for a new product, when there are already similar products, in order to penetrate the market. Once the product is established, the price will increase.
- **Price skimming** – Charging a high price for a product that is new and perhaps a bit different. Customers are happy to pay the high price as they associate the product with prestige or status, for example the new version of an Apple iPhone.
- **Destroyer pricing** – Setting a low price with the aim of destroying the competition. Once the competition has been destroyed the business can raise the price again as there will be no other businesses supplying the product.

> **EXAM TIP**
>
> You should be able to name and describe pricing strategies and give examples of products being priced in different ways.

Promotion and advertising

Product **promotion** involves persuading customers to buy the product using a variety of techniques, for example free entry into competitions, money-off vouchers, discounts, BOGOF, free sampling. These all allow the customer to be persuaded into buying by thinking that they are getting a good deal.

Advertising involves giving out information about the product. There are many ways to advertise: television and radio, billboards and posters, cinemas, newspapers and magazines, flyers and leaflets, websites, email, text messaging, sponsorship and celebrity endorsements.

The method chosen by a business will depend on the target market, how much money they are prepared to spend, what their competitors are doing and what type of product they are selling. More and more businesses are concentrating on personal marketing – getting the message directly to the customer.

Ethical marketing

The growth of media and personal electronic devices has led to an increase in the number of people who can be targeted directly by advertising. However not all individuals want or need this type of approach. Also, as advertising and promotion have become much more sophisticated there is a growing need to ensure that they are ethical, i.e. that the promotion is honest and not just aiming to make profits at the expense of individuals. Ethical marketing avoids businesses making claims that products are going to change people's lives and protects vulnerable groups such as the elderly or those on low incomes.

Apply Your Knowledge

Be advertising aware! Check out the different ways in which advertisements appear in your daily life, such as billboards, cinema, the back of buses. Can you remember advertising slogans or songs and the product being advertised?

Develop Your Skills

1. Check out prices in your local supermarket or store. How many special offers can you see? How many products have 'buy one get one free' (BOGOF) offers?

2. Newly launched products get lots of attention. What pricing strategies have been used for tablet computers?

Quick Test

1. Name and describe two pricing strategies.
2. Give two methods of promotion.
3. List two methods of advertising.

The marketing mix: 3

This chapter looks at the fourth element of the marketing mix – place.

Place

Place refers to how the product gets to the consumer and where it is sold. The place element of the marketing mix has changed considerably in the last 10 years.

Products get to consumers in a variety of different ways – often referred to as channels of distribution. This means how the product is transported and distributed. There are four main channels.

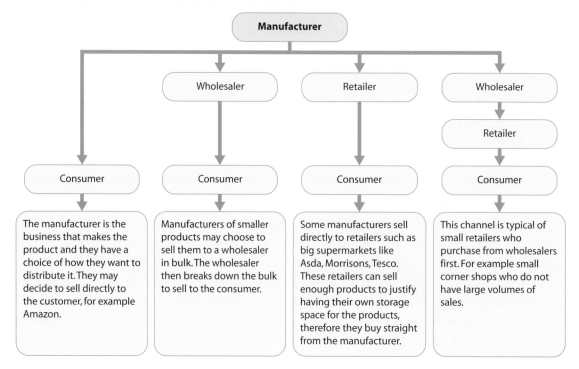

The manufacturer is the business that makes the product and they have a choice of how they want to distribute it. They may decide to sell directly to the customer, for example Amazon.

Manufacturers of smaller products may choose to sell them to a wholesaler in bulk. The wholesaler then breaks down the bulk to sell to the consumer.

Some manufacturers sell directly to retailers such as big supermarkets like Asda, Morrisons, Tesco. These retailers can sell enough products to justify having their own storage space for the products, therefore they buy straight from the manufacturer.

This channel is typical of small retailers who purchase from wholesalers first. For example small corner shops who do not have large volumes of sales.

Place also refers to where the products are sold. For example:

- shops
- e-commerce websites
- markets
- TV shopping channels
- vending machines
- catalogues
- newspapers and magazines
- home shopping parties
- telephone ordering

got it? ☐ ☐ ☐

Business location

The location of a business is important. There are a number of factors that influence business location.

- **Competition** – Businesses may decide to locate either near to their competitors or in a completely different location. Locating beside competitors means that customers can make immediate choices and comparisons. Locating away from the competition can mean that more customers will be attracted to your products.

- **Availability of resources/premises –** Businesses will want to locate beside resources, such as a pool of labour, good transport links, suitable premises, near to customers. They will want premises that are not too expensive but are suitable for their purposes. In many cases businesses will want space for customer parking. Stores like Homebase and B&Q need parking for their customers who are usually buying large bulky items so very often choose a retail park outside town which is easy for customers to get to.

- **Government assistance** – Some businesses locate in areas where the government is prepared to offer assistance and support. For example in Scotland regional selective assistance is offered for locating in certain areas. Grants may also be available as well as reduced rates and loans.

Apply Your Knowledge

Find out how Internet sales have changed the way that customers buy products. Research this using news websites.

Develop Your Skills

Find out about Regional Selective Assistance grants for businesses to locate in certain areas of Scotland. Go to http://www.scottish-enterprise.com/fund-your-business; here you will find details of grants available for areas in Scotland.

Quick Test

1. Describe two channels of distribution.
2. Describe why some businesses use a wholesaler.

What is operations?

The operations function

Operations involves making raw materials into finished products. This is usually called production. Operations also involves managing stock control and supplies so that the business gets good quality materials at a good price.

The operations function is often shown as a diagram:

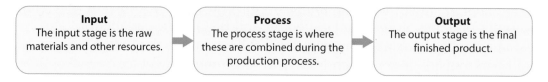

| **Input** The input stage is the raw materials and other resources. | → | **Process** The process stage is where these are combined during the production process. | → | **Output** The output stage is the final finished product. |

Choosing a supplier

Manufacturers want to make sure that they receive good quality raw materials in order to produce their products. Therefore the following factors are important in choosing a supplier.

- The price charged by the supplier.
- The quality of the raw materials.
- The time it takes for raw materials to be delivered.
- The cost of transporting the raw materials.
- The reliability and reputation of the supplier.

EXAM TIP

Any delays in the delivery of raw materials will mean delays in production that may cost the business money.

Stock management

Manufacturers can operate two types of stock control systems. They can hold stocks of raw materials in their premises or they can operate a just-in-time system.

Storing stock requires the business to have suitable stock warehouses or stock rooms. These must be dry and well-ventilated and appropriate for storing stock. They must also be secure in order to avoid theft. **Overstocking** can lead to cash flow problems if the stock is held for too long and goes out of date or fashion, or simply does not sell quick enough in order to bring in cash. Most businesses operate a system of setting stock levels in order to avoid this.

- **Maximum stock** is the greatest amount of each item that will be stored. This level is based on regular usage.

- **Minimum stock** is the lowest level that the item is allowed to fall to before production could be halted and risking customers going elsewhere. This is also based on regular usage.
- **The re-order level** is the level that stock can fall to before a new batch of raw materials will be re-ordered. This is based on regular usage and the time it takes to order in and receive the new stock.

Understocking can lead to loss of profit if customers go to other suppliers.

Just-in-time stock control

Some businesses operate a system of just-in-time stock control or just-in-time production. Raw materials are ordered as and when they are needed and they are delivered regularly to be used immediately. This avoids the need for expensive stock warehouses and stock rooms. However it relies on suppliers being on time with deliveries. There can be problems during periods of bad weather or transport strikes.

Computerised stock control

The use of computerised stock control systems allows businesses to have more control over their stock. These can be very simple spreadsheets, which record stock in, out and the balance; or they can be sophisticated database or bespoke systems that allow management to closely monitor stock levels. Computerised stock control systems will enable the business to do the following:

- print stock lists showing the balance of each item
- automatically re-order stock when re-order level is reached
- record details of suppliers and their delivery times
- automatically update stock balance after sales when linked to electronic point of sale (EPOS) systems
- update prices of stock quickly and easily

Apply Your Knowledge

Why do shops have sales? Why do they sell off their stock at a reduced price?

EXAM TIP

Control of stock is very important for any business as they can lose money if there is too much or too little.

Quick Test

1. Identify three features of a good supplier.
2. Explain what just-in-time stock control means.
3. Explain what maximum stock means.
4. Describe the advantages to a business of using EPOS.

Production

Labour or capital intensive production

The production of finished goods can be either **labour intensive** or **capital intensive**. Labour intensive means that people use their skills and knowledge to produce handcrafted products. Capital intensive means that machines are mostly used – normally in factories with production lines. This can also include robots and fully automated systems where there are no humans involved at all.

Type of Production	Benefits	Costs
Labour intensive	Humans can use their skills and abilities and their initiative.	Humans are expensive and can be absent from work, which costs money.
Capital intensive	Machines can work 24 hours a day. Machines can do boring repetitive jobs with a high degree of accuracy.	Machines are expensive to install and maintain. When machines break down production stops.

Methods of production

EXAM TIP

You should be able to name and describe and give examples of job, batch and flow production.

There are three main methods of production – job, batch and flow.

Job production

This method of production involves a unique product being made exactly to customer requirements such as a bespoke piece of jewelry. It is sometimes referred to as 'one off' production. The product is made from start to finish by a skilled worker, usually by hand. Because the product is unique, high prices can be charged by the producer. However the cost of wages for making the product can also be high.

Advantages of job production	Disadvantages of job production
Products can be made exactly to customer requirements.	The products can take a long time to make.
High prices can be charged.	Does not usually involve bulk orders.
Products are usually of good quality.	Wages may be very high.

Batch production

Batch production involves products being made together at the same time that are identical. Subsequent batches are similar – but they may not be identical because of slight changes in the raw materials. Many food products are made in batches, for example chocolate, crisps, bread, ice-cream. The products are usually stamped with the date and time and batch number. They also have a 'use by' or 'best before' date to guide the consumer. Other products that are made in batches include wallpaper and paint. Batch production involves both people and machines.

Advantages of batch production	Disadvantages of batch production
Products can be produced more cheaply than with job production.	If there is a problem the whole batch may be wasted.
Batches can be changed to keep up-to-date with customer requirements.	Machinery or equipment may have to be changed between batches and this may be time-consuming.

Flow production

Flow production involves identical products such as cars being made continuously on a production line. The role of employees is usually to maintain the machinery and intervene when machines break down.

Advantages of flow production	Disadvantages of flow production
Products can be made in high volumes at a relatively low cost.	Products are all the same with no individuality.
The use of machinery is efficient as it can run 24 hours per day.	If machinery breaks down, production will be halted.
Raw materials can be purchased in bulk, leading to cost savings.	There can be quality issues if quality control is not used properly.

Apply Your Knowledge

Flow production can be cheap and produces lots of products that are exactly the same – but what is an employee's role in this? Do you think they enjoy their job on a production line?

Quick Test

1. Explain the difference between capital intensive and labour intensive production.
2. Identify two examples of products that are produced using job production.
3. Describe one advantage and one disadvantage of batch production.
4. Explain why products are cheaper to produce using flow production.

Quality

What is quality?

Quality means different things to different people. In terms of production, customers usually want value for money – they want quality that is consistent with the price they pay for the product. Products that are higher in price are usually better quality.

Quality products should be safe and fit for purpose. They should last for the period of time expected at purchase. An expensive pair of shoes will be expected to last longer than a pair of flip flops.

A quality product involves the following:

- using high-quality raw materials
- training employees regularly and to a high standard
- using up-to-date machinery and equipment
- using packaging that is appropriate
- the product being delivered on time
- the product is produced to quality standards, e.g. to the Kitemark system

> **EXAM TIP**
>
> Businesses will produce good-quality products if they implement quality production systems.

Costs and benefits of quality

To ensure good quality, businesses have to be prepared to incur the following costs: higher raw material costs, costs of training staff, costs of applying for quality awards.

It is accepted wisdom that the benefits of good quality outweigh the costs in the long term. If businesses take steps to ensure good-quality products they will gain the following benefits: customers will be happy with the products and will therefore return to buy more; happy customers will increase the reputation of the business; employees will be more satisfied and more motivated in their jobs; good-quality products will reduce waste; profits can be increased.

Ensuring quality

Quality circles

This involves groups of employees coming together with the management in order to discuss issues of quality. They may come up with suggestions on improving quality or they may train each other in improving quality. The emphasis is usually on how to improve the quality of the final product.

Quality control

This involves checking products to make sure they meet the standards expected. If a product fails the quality check it is discarded or recycled back into the production process. Quality control can be wasteful if it is only carried out at the end of the production process. It would be more efficient to check quality at various stages during the production process.

Quality assurance

This involves checking products at more regular intervals during the production process and trying to avoid problems happening in the first place. If quality assurance checks are carried out employees are more confident that the completed product will be acceptable. This reduces waste overall and makes employees more satisfied with their jobs.

Quality management

This involves every employee in the organisation ensuring that quality is built-in at every stage of the production process. It ensures that quality raw materials are purchased from reliable suppliers. Any errors or problems in the production process are eliminated and the failure rate of finished products is very low indeed.

All staff, including office staff, are involved in the quality process. Often organisations have quality awards for their high standards, for example Investors in People, charter marks and the BSI Kitemark. Customers know, therefore, that the product is of good quality.

Apply Your Knowledge

Do some customers expect higher quality standards than others? How does a business take this into account?

Develop Your Skills

Investigate any products that have been recalled because of problems in production, for example horsemeat in products from major retailers in 2013. How could this have happened?

Quick Test

1. Describe two features of a quality product.
2. Describe quality assurance.
3. Describe quality management.
4. List the benefits to a business of good-quality products.

What are ethical and environmental issues?: 1

These are the ways in which businesses behave in order to achieve their goals and objectives. Trying to make profits is not always easy. Businesses have high costs to pay in a competitive market. Some businesses may be tempted to cut down on their costs by adopting unethical business practices and not caring for the environment.

The supply chain

Many businesses carefully select their suppliers to make sure that any raw materials have been produced or obtained in an ethical way. For example, the growth of fair trade products in the UK ensures that farmers in developing countries get a fair share of the profits. Sometimes raw materials are selected by businesses because they have been grown organically or they are not genetically modified in any way. Suppliers may be chosen because they can prove that no child workers have been involved or that they pay their employees a decent wage.

The FAIRTRADE Mark is an independent certification label owned by Fairtrade International. When you see the Mark on products it means farmers and workers in developing countries have received a fair and stable price as well as the Fairtrade premium, which they choose how to invest in their businesses and communities.

Businesses may also select their suppliers based on their reputation for health and safety concerns. If a supplier ignores health and safety or welfare issues they risk losing business as well as being shut down by the government.

If businesses import cheap raw materials or finished products from other countries they risk losing British-based customers who believe that cheap imports are poor quality and that British employees are losing their jobs to overseas suppliers.

The environment

EXAM TIP

Many businesses are marketing their products as 'environmentally friendly' to try and win more customers.

The government has actively encouraged care for the environment for decades. Businesses and individuals are more aware of potential damage to the environment. The main environmental issues are:

- **Waste** – Businesses produce waste naturally but this cannot be 'dumped' into the environment, especially if it is harmful in any way. Businesses have to find ways of reducing waste, recycling or disposing of it in a responsible way.
- **Emissions** – Greenhouse gases and emissions have to be reduced in order to prevent further damage to the environment. Responsible businesses use filters and screens to reduce smoke and chemical emissions.
- **Sustainable development** – All production uses raw materials that have come from the earth in some way. Many businesses now operate a policy of sustainable development where they replace raw materials that they are using. For example trees are replanted regularly in this country to make sure that there are supplies of wood in the future.

Apply Your Knowledge

Have you purchased Fairtrade products in school or in the supermarket? Why do you think customers buy Fairtrade products? Are Fairtrade products of a similar standard to supermarket brands?

Develop Your Skills

Go to www.fairtrade.org.uk and find out more about Fairtrade products available in the UK.

Quick Test

1. Explain why it is important for businesses to choose an environmentally friendly supplier.
2. Give two main ways in which the environment can be damaged.
3. What is sustainable development?

What are ethical and environmental issues?: 2

Recycling and packaging

Recycling

Both households and businesses now make huge efforts to recycle waste and packaging. Recycling is becoming increasingly important and has many advantages.

- Waste materials can be made into new products. This means that the world's natural resources have a chance to recover and be renewed.

- Recycled materials can help to save energy in the production process as products do not require new raw materials.

- Recycling helps to protect the environment as greenhouse gas emissions can be reduced and there is less need to keep mining and quarrying for new raw materials.

- If waste materials are recycled there is no need to dump them into landfill sites, which can produce and take up space in our countryside.

Costs of recycling	Benefits of recycling
Costs of providing bins, bags etc.	Helps to protect natural resources.
Costs of personnel to collect waste.	Saves energy.
Costs of transport to sites.	Protects the natural environment.
Costs of providing recycling sites.	Fewer landfill sites.

Packaging

Packaging is really important for the final product in any industry. Packaging helps to protect the product during transportation and while on the shelves. Packaging also helps to sell the product if it is a luxury item like perfume and makeup.

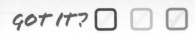

The growth in fast food and home delivery food has seen an increase in packaging, which not only uses up natural resources but can also cause litter issues, especially in large towns and cities.

Packaging has been reduced in many common household goods and fast foods.

Costs of reducing packaging	Benefits of reducing packaging
Products may get damaged on route to customers.	Less packaging means less waste and fewer resources being used up.
Customers may think that the products are inferior as the packaging can be very attractive.	Less packaging means less litter being dumped, which means that more time can be spent on recycling.

Apply Your Knowledge

Use the following websites to help you with the questions below:

www.recyclenow.com

www.greenchoices.org

1. What steps have businesses taken to reduce packaging and to recycle more waste?

2. Research some products which use excess packaging.

Develop Your Skills

1. What advice would you give to your family about purchasing products with packaging?

2. What advice would you give to your family about recycling in your household?

Quick Test

1.   Give two costs and two benefits of recycling.

2.   Give one cost and one benefit of reducing packaging.

Technology: 1

Technology in business is constantly changing. Businesses have to try and keep up with developments in order to stay competitive and to meet customers' needs.

Computer-aided design (CAD)

CAD is the name given to software programs that allow the user to create drawings, plans and blueprints using computers. Previously these drawings would have been done by hand. Architects, graphic designers, engineers and designers can now produce drawings and plans in both 2D and 3D that will allow the client to see images of what the final product will look like. This could be a new kitchen, new house, electrical product etc.

Computer-aided manufacture (CAM)

Computer-aided manufacture (CAM) is the name given to manufacturing systems that are automated. The machinery and robots used in the production process are controlled by a computer. The computer gives instructions that can be changed at short notice if necessary, or to facilitate small changes in the design. The use of CAM allows precision in the manufacturing process and it also reduces the number of employees required.

EXAM TIP

You must be able to describe how the technology used improves how the business operates.

Electronic point of sale (EPOS)

EPOS is more commonly known as an electronic checkout. Large stores and supermarkets use EPOS at the point where customers hand over their money to buy goods and services. The EPOS system is controlled by computer and it allows a receipt to be given to the customer, with all the details of the purchase listed along with other information such as special offers, discount vouchers etc. The EPOS system scans the barcodes on the products, which looks up the price of the

item and deducts the item from the total stock balance. This means that at the end of each trading day the business can print out lists of all the stock sold during that time. Many EPOS systems have touch screens, which makes it very easy and quick for the operator to complete the transaction for the customer.

EPOS can also gather valuable market research data. The system can produce reports to show which items have sold quickly and those that are not popular. Prices can be changed at any time on the system so the business can track how sensitive demand is to changes in price.

Apply Your Knowledge

EPOS has changed the way retailers operate but how does it improve the experience for customers?

Develop Your Skills

Examine any products that you have bought recently. Can you see the bar code information?

- What does the business do with this bar code information?
- How does this help with stock control?

Quick Test

1. Give a description of CAD.
2. Give a description of CAM.
3. Explain EPOS and how it helps with stock control.

Technology: 2

Technology has transformed the way in which businesses and customers communicate with one another and the way in which customers shop.

Electronic surveys

Electronic surveys are growing in popularity. More and more businesses and organisations are gathering market research information online. This is more immediate and cost-effective than sending out paper questionnaires to be returned by post. Online surveys usually do not take long to complete. They are often included as 'pop ups' on a website, but can also be constructed on dedicated survey websites such as Survey Monkey. The results of the survey can be analysed online and the information is gathered very quickly. Electronic  surveys can be used for customers and employees; employee satisfaction surveys can be carried out quickly and confidentially.

Electronic surveys can be carried out in the following ways.

- Sending emails to customers with a link to a website.
- Feedback forms on websites.
- Sending SMS messages, asking for customers to provide ratings by text.
- Using survey websites such as Survey Monkey.

Electronic surveys are here to stay. Businesses and organisations will continue to use them to collect valuable market research data.

Internet advertising

Internet advertising has grown considerably since the early 2000s. Businesses can advertise via their own websites but also through hyperlinks from other websites and through search engines.

- A global audience can be reached on a regular basis.
- New animation and graphic techniques means that Internet advertisements now look like TV advertisements.
- Internet advertising can be targeted directly at customers depending on what they are browsing.

- Customers can be reached in many different locations, for example on mobile tablets.
- Smartphones also allow customers to be targeted directly on a daily basis.
- Social networking sites provide opportunities to target specific groups regularly.
- Customers can be targeted for recommended purchases depending on what they have bought in the past.

E-commerce direct sales

Customers have choices of where and how they want to shop. Online sales have grown considerably and this has a knock-on effect on high street sales.

Customers can order goods online and have them delivered quickly to their homes, often with free delivery. Most high street retailers have websites with the same (or more) products available online. They also provide secure online payment systems so customers are confident in their online purchases. The same guarantees exist for online purchases as for shop purchases.

There has also been a growth in grocery shopping online. Most of the main supermarkets now offer online shopping with delivery at pre-arranged times so that the food does not perish. Customers can shop easily, with their regular purchases already stored on the website to speed up the process.

Apply Your Knowledge

What are the features of a good website? What should be included for customers' ease of use?

EXAM TIP

Customers can now make online purchases sites using a PC, laptop, tablet or smartphone.

Develop Your Skills

Have you completed an online survey? Was it easy to do? Find out if any members of your household have completed online surveys recently.

Quick Test

1. Describe two advantages on electronic surveys for a business.
2. Describe two advantages of Internet advertising.
3. Describe two advantages of online shopping for both the business and the customer.

Quick Test Answers

Satisfying wants (page 13)

1. **Describe the difference between needs and wants.**
   Needs are things we must have, such as food and clothing, wants are things we would like to have, such as cars and computers.

2. **Describe how wealth is created by a business.**
   Wealth is created by a business by adding value at each stage of production, e.g. a furniture maker adds value by creating a table from trees that have been cut down.

Sectors of industry and the economy (page 15)

1. **Name the three sectors of industry.**
   Primary, Secondary and Tertiary.

2. **Give an example of an organisation that operates in the public sector.**
   Schools, hospitals, council-run leisure centres.

What is customer service? (page 17)

1. **Describe two ways that businesses can offer customers good service.**
   Staff training, loyalty cards, bonus offers, setting service standards, offering guarantees.

2. **Give three reasons for offering good customer service.**
   Increased customer loyalty, increased sales and profits, a good reputation, increased competitiveness, increased staff morale and effectiveness.

3. **Explain why it is important to train staff in customer service.**
   So that all staff treat customers in the same way and a standard can be set. Nothing is left to chance. So that staff are confident in their ability to deal with customers.

Complaints, refunds and guarantees (page 19)

1. **Explain the drawbacks of offering guarantees to customers.**
The business must make sure that it can carry out the terms of the guarantee, otherwise customers will not be happy.

2. **How can a business make sure that customers' complaints are handled correctly?**
By having a published complaints procedure so that customers know what to do. Also by training staff.

3. **What should a business do if customers are constantly complaining?**
Make sure that staff are properly trained. Look at the quality of the products or services to see if they need improved. Carry out market research to identify the problem.

Private sector businesses and public sector organisations (page 21)

1. **Explain the difference between limited and unlimited liability.**
Limited liability means that an investor in a business can only lose the share that they have put in if the company goes bankrupt. Unlimited liability means that the owner can also lose all their personal possessions if the business goes bankrupt. For example, a sole trader has unlimited liability.

2. **Describe the ownership of a private limited company.**
A private limited company is owned by shareholders. However, shares are not available to buy on the stock exchange.

3. **Describe how profits are distributed in a partnership.**
Profits are split among partners according to the ratio they agreed in the original partnership agreement.

The third sector, charities and social enterprises (page 23)

1. **What are the main aims of third sector organisations?**
   They aim to provide advice, support and education for a particular cause or charity. They raise awareness and funding from grants, donations, lottery etc.

2. **Explain why an entrepreneur might start-up a social enterprise business.**
   In order to benefit their local community. In order to develop their skills and expertise in an area that they are comfortable with.

What are business objectives? (page 25)

1. **Describe two objectives of a private sector business.**
   To make a profit, to survive, to grow, to provide a good product or service.

2. **Describe the main objective of public sector organisations.**
   To provide a service to the public.

3. **Describe two objectives of third sector organisations.**
   To provide advice and support to the local community. To raise awareness of a particular cause.

4. **Describe how a social enterprise differs from a private limited company.**
   A social enterprise is primarily concerned with helping the community and although it can make a profit there are no shareholders. A private limited company has shareholders and a board of directors appointed to run the company on behalf of the shareholders.

Factors that affect a business: 1 (page 27)

1. **Describe how the government can affect the day-to-day running of a business.**
   The government can introduce laws that affect every business in the UK. Businesses have to comply with these laws and this usually costs them money.

2. **Apart from bad weather, list the other environmental factors that can affect a business.**
   Pollution, and waste disposal, recycling.

Factors that affect a business: 2 (page 29)

1. **Explain the difference between internal and external factors.**
   Internal factors are events and situations *within* the business that affect its performance overall. External factors are *outwith* the business.

2. **Give the actions a business must take if it installs new technology.**
   The business must ensure that the technology is up-to-date and that all staff are trained in the use of the technology.

Stakeholders: 1 (page 31)

1. **Name two internal and two external stakeholders.**
   Internal – Owners (including shareholders), employees, managers
   External – Customers, suppliers, banks, the local community (including pressure groups), the Government

2. **What interest does the local community have in a business?**
   The local community will want jobs provided and also want the community to be free from pollution.

3. **What interest does the Government have in a business?**
   The Government is interested in the business paying tax and keeping within the law.

Stakeholders: 2 (page 33)

1. **Outline actions that employees can take which may affect the business.**
   Employees can choose to work hard and produce good-quality products and services. They can also take industrial action.

2. **Describe the consequences for a business if they have to change supplier.**
   They may have to pay higher prices or accept goods of inferior quality.

3. **Describe the main actions that customers can take if they are not happy with a business.**
   Go to another business, complain, spread the word to other customers that they are not happy.

Recruitment (page 35)

1. **Compare internal and external recruitment.**
   Internal recruitment is when a vacancy is filled from within the business. External recruitment is when a vacancy is advertised on the open market and the new employee comes from outwith the business.

2. **Identify three pieces of information contained in a job description.**
   Job title, hours of work, rate of pay, holidays, duties and responsibilities.

3. **Describe what a recruitment agency would use a person specification for.**
   To cross-check the skills and qualities of applicants for a job against those in the person specification.

4. **Identify three places where jobs can be advertised externally.**
   Internet websites, newspapers, job centres.

Selection of employees (page 37)

1. **Give the advantages of using an interview as the only means of selecting a candidate for a job.**
   The interview can give an in-depth insight into the candidate. They get to outline in detail their strengths and weaknesses.

2. **Describe the disadvantages of using personality tests as a means of selecting candidates.**
   Not all candidates fit neatly into the categories of personality tests. Candidates can be nervous because of the 'test' and not answer correctly. Candidates can be dishonest in their answers.

3. **Describe the role an assessment centre plays in the recruitment process.**
   The centre advertises the vacancy on behalf of the business, they collect and sort applications, check them against the criteria and set up interviews and other selection procedures on behalf of the business.

Training of employees (page 39)

1. **Explain the difference between on-the-job and off-the-job training.**
   On-the-job training takes place at the place of work and usually involves demonstrations, job rotation etc. Off-the-job training involves going to an external training centre or college and being trained by experts or lecturers.

2. **Describe two costs and two benefits of on-the-job training.**
   Costs – Time can be lost to do the employee's job, employees may feel awkward being trained by each other.
   Benefits – Training is specific to the job, no time is lost away from the work place.

3. **Describe two methods of employee training that could be done off-the-job.**
   Lectures at college, role play at college, multimedia DVDs.

4. **Describe what induction training is.**
   Training that is offered to new employees in a business for them to find out about the business and the new job.

Motivating and retaining employees (page 41)

1. **Explain what 'double time' is when paying employees.**
   Double time is the rate of hourly pay multiplied by two.

2. **Define the phrase 'non-financial rewards'.**
   These are additional benefits given to employees but not in the form of cash.

3. **Give two examples of non-financial rewards.**
   Company car, pension contributions, luncheon vouchers, child care vouchers etc.

4. **Describe the role of a works council.**
   A committee of employees and management that discusses areas of the business that they are concerned about so that everyone is working positively towards the goals of the business.

Trade unions (page 43)

1. **What is a trade union and what does it do?**
   A trade union is an organization made up of employees in the workplace. It provides help and advice to members and negotiates for pay and conditions.

2. **Why does industrial action sometimes take place?**
   Because employees and management have a disagreement which they cannot resolve.

3. **What is the difference between a strike and a sit-in?**
   A strike is when employees refuse to attend for work, whereas a sit-in is when employees occupy the work place and do not go home.

Legislation (page 45)

1. **Describe the duties of employees under the Health and Safety at Work Act.**
   To ensure that they protect themselves and others in the work place. To ensure that they use any items given to them for health and safety.

2. **Explain two ways that employees may be discriminated against at work.**
   On the grounds of sex, race, religion, disability.

3. **Describe two features of the Data Protection Act.**
   The data must be held according to certain principles, for example it must be accurate and up-to-date, it must be obtained fairly and lawfully and it must be protected against misuse.

Sources of finance: 1 (page 47)

1. **Name three sources of finance for a sole trader.**
   Own savings, family and friends, bank loan.

2. **Explain what a bank overdraft is.**
   A short term loan from the bank where you are allowed to withdraw more than you have in the bank. Interest is charged on the overdraft.

3. **Describe what a mortgage is usually given for.**
   Purchase of a property or premises.

Sources of finance: 2 (page 49)

1. **How does the government obtain finance for spending on the economy?**
   They raise taxes from businesses and individuals.

2. **What is VAT?**
   Value Added Tax – this is added to purchases made by consumers.

3. **Identify one method of obtaining finance in the third sector.**
   Gifts, donations, grants from the Government, trading activities e.g. coffee shop.

Costs and the break even point (page 51)

1. **Describe fixed costs.**
   Costs that do not change as output changes.

2. **Describe variable costs.**
   Costs that do change as output changes.

3. **Give one example of a fixed cost and one example of a variable cost.**
   Fixed costs – rent, manager's salary, council tax. Variable costs – wages, raw materials.

4. **Explain the break even point.**
   The point at which neither a profit nor a loss is being made.

Cash budgeting (page 53)

1. **Give two advantages of preparing a cash budget.**
   Business can plan its income and expenditure. Can see at a glance where they may be financial problems in the future.

2. **Identify two expenses for a business.**
   Stationery for the office, rent, telephone bill, electricity, employee wages etc.

3. **Describe two ways in which a business could solve cash flow problems.**
   Obtaining a loan or overdraft from the bank. Raising extra capital. Cutting back on projected expenses. Asking suppliers or creditors for extra time to pay bills. Spreading the cost of purchase of assets, for example hire purchase or lease. Cut down on purchases of stock, e.g. finding a cheaper supplier. Encourage customers to pay on time, for example by offering discounts.

4. **Explain how a spreadsheet can help to improve cash flow.**
   Formulas can be entered into the spreadsheet to perform calculations. Changes can be made to figures and the formula will automatically update all the figures.

Profit statement (page 55)

1. **Describe what gross profit is.**
   Gross profit is the profit made from buying and selling goods and services. It is calculated by subtracting cost of goods sold away from sales.

2. **Describe what net profit is.**
   Net profit is gross profit less expenses of the business.

3. **Give two production costs.**
   Cost of raw materials and cost of labour.

4. **List two overhead costs.**
   Rent of the factory, supervisors' salaries.

New technology: 1 (page 57)

1. **Describe two ways that spreadsheets can be used to help business managers.**
   Spreadsheets can be used to prepare cash budgets and manage cash flow allowing business managers to make decisions quickly.

2. **List two ways that businesses can use technology to train employees.**
   Online videos, e-learning courses, DVDs.

New technology: 2 (page 59)

1. **Explain how online testing can save time for employers recruiting candidates.**
   Candidates who are not suitable according to the test do not have to be called for interview.

2. **Describe the advantages to employers of online applications.**
   Applications can be located quickly on the website, candidates can be emailed interview times quickly.

Who are your customers? (page 61)

1. **Explain why businesses need to know who their customers are.**
   So that they can target their customers by producing goods and services that they want.

2. **What is meant by market segments?**
   Specific groups of people in the market who all want similar things e.g. teenagers.

3. **Why is it important to target specific market segments?**
   To avoid wasting resources and to make sure that products get to the correct market segment.

4. **What products would you aim at children aged 5–8 years?**
   Toys, books, DVDs, sweets, electronic games, bicycles etc.

Market research: 1 (page 63)

1. **Explain what is meant by market research.**
   Finding out what customers want by asking them directly or gathering information from other sources.

2. **How does market research help a business?**
   It helps to know what customers want so that resources are not wasted providing other products.

3. **Why would a researcher carry out an interview instead of a postal survey?**
   To see the facial expression and to get to know the interviewee better.

4. **What is the main benefit of field research?**
   You can get immediate answers to questions and people will be more honest face-to-face.

Market research: 2 (page 65)

1. **What is desk research?**
Finding information from existing or secondary sources.

2. **Outline two methods of desk research.**
Using government statistics that have already been gathered, using websites with relevant information, using books, magazines etc.

3. **What is the main benefit of desk research?**
The information is usually available free of charge.

The marketing mix: 1 (page 67)

1. **Describe three stages of the product development process.**
An idea is generated. Market research is undertaken. Product research is undertaken. A prototype is developed. The prototype is tested on the market. Adaptations are made on the basis of market testing. The product is launched.

2. **Name the four stages of the product life cycle.**
Introduction, Growth, Maturity, Decline

3. **Suggest two ways that the product life cycle can be extended.**
Changing the product in some way, changing the packaging, altering the price, changing the place where it is sold.

The marketing mix: 2 (page 69)

1. **Name and describe two pricing strategies.**
Cost plus pricing, penetration pricing, destroyer pricing.

2. **Give two methods of promotion.**
Free entry into competitions, money-off vouchers, discounts, BOGOF, free sampling

3. **List two methods of advertising**
Television and radio, billboards and posters, cinemas, newspapers and magazines, flyers and leaflets, websites, email, text messaging, sponsorship, celebrity endorsements

The marketing mix: 3 (page 71)

1. **Describe two channels of distribution.**
   Manufacturer to wholesaler to retailer to consumer.
   Manufacturer to retailer to consumer.

2. **Describe why some businesses use a wholesaler.**
   The wholesaler breaks down the bulk of the product to sell to the retailer in smaller amounts.

What is operations? (page 73)

1. **Identify three features of a good supplier.**
   Delivers on time, has good quality materials, charges good prices.

2. **Explain what just-in-time stock control means.**
   Raw materials are delivered just in time for the production process rather than holding large stocks.

3. **Explain what maximum stock means.**
   The maximum amount of stock that a business holds at any one time. Usually depending on how much they use and how much storage space they have.

4. **Describe the advantages to a business of using EPOS.**
   Stock levels can be monitored easily. Stock can be re-ordered automatically. Stock lists can be printed regularly.

Production (page 75)

1. **Explain the difference between capital intensive and labour intensive production.**
   Capital intensive uses mostly machines in the production process, labour intensive uses mostly people in the production process.

2. **Identify two examples of products that are produced using job production.**
   Suits, wedding dresses, birthday cakes.

3. **Describe one advantage and one disadvantage of batch production.**
   Advantage – products can be produced more cheaply than with job production.
   Disadvantage – if there is a problem the whole batch may be wasted.

4. **Explain why products are cheaper to produce using flow production.**
   Production volumes are high therefore the unit cost of production is lower.

Quality (page 77)

1. **Describe two features of a quality product.**
   Quality products should be safe and fit for purpose. They should last for the period of time expected at purchase.

2. **Describe quality assurance.**
   Checking products at more regular intervals during the production process and trying to avoid problems happening in the first place.

3. **Describe quality management.**
   This involves every employee in the organisation ensuring that quality is built-in at each and every stage of the production process.

4. **List the benefits to a business of good quality products.**
   Customers will be happy with the products and therefore will return to buy more.
   Happy customers will increase the reputation of the business.
   Employees will be more satisfied and more motivated in their jobs.
   Good-quality products will reduce waste. Profits can be increased

What are ethical and environmental issues?: 1 (page 79)

1. **Explain why it is important for businesses to choose an environmentally friendly supplier.**
   To make sure that any raw materials have been produced or obtained in an ethical way.

2. **Give two main ways in which the environment can be damaged.**
   Greenhouse gas emissions and illegal dumping of waste.

3. **What is sustainable development?**
   When businesses replace raw materials that they are constantly using e.g. replanting trees.

What are ethical and environmental issues?: 2 (page 81)

1. **Give two costs and two benefits of recycling.**
   Costs - providing bins, bags etc., wages of personnel to collect waste, transport, providing recycling sites.

   Benefits - helps to protect natural resources, saves energy, protects the natural environment, fewer landfill sites.

2. **Give one cost and one benefit of reducing packaging.**
   Reducing packaging can increase the risk of products becoming damaged however reducing packaging can help protect the environment by reducing waste.

Technology: 1 (page 83)

1. **Give a description of CAD.**
   Computer-aided design where software is used in the design process.

2. **Give a description of CAM.**
   Computer-aided manufacture where computers are used in the production process.

3. **Explain EPOS and how it helps with stock control.**
   Electronic point of sale. When products are sold and 'bleeped' through the cash register the stock automatically updates and re-orders.

Technology: 2 (page 85)

1. **Describe two advantages of electronic surveys for a business.**
   The results of the survey can be analysed online and the information is gathered very quickly. Electronic surveys can be used for customers and employees; employee satisfaction surveys can be carried out quickly and confidentially.

2. **Describe two advantages of Internet advertising.**
   A global audience can be reached on a regular basis. New animation and graphic techniques means that Internet ads now look like TV ads. Internet advertising can be targeted directly at customers depending on what they are browsing. Internet advertising is professional, eye-catching, and interesting.

3. **Describe two advantages of online shopping for both the business and the customer.**
   Business – increases sales because of online shopping, easy to target new customers on internet websites.
   Customer – have a choice of where and when they want to shop, products delivered to their homes, secure online payment systems so shoppers do not have to worry.